THE WHOLE CHILD

Raising Emotionally Intelligent Kids in a World That Forgot How

---

Ken Konet, M.Ed., MBA

Copyright

Published in the United States by Humbolton, LLC

First Edition

ISBN: 978-1-966703-29-7 [Paperback]

For permission, inquiries, or bulk orders, contact: Humbolton.com

---

Disclaimer

The content of this book is intended for educational and informational purposes only. It is not a substitute for professional medical, psychological, psychiatric, or therapeutic advice, diagnosis, or treatment. The strategies, frameworks, and information presented in these pages reflect the author's research, professional experience, and perspective, and are not intended to replace the guidance of a licensed mental health professional, physician, pediatrician, or other qualified healthcare provider.

If you or your child are experiencing significant emotional, behavioral, or mental health challenges, please seek the advice of a qualified professional. Do not disregard, delay, or discontinue professional medical or psychological care based on anything you have read in this book.

Every child and family is unique. What works for one may not work for another. The author and publisher make no guarantees regarding outcomes and assume no liability for any loss, damage, or disruption, personal, psychological, financial, or otherwise, arising from the application of any information contained in this book.

If you are in crisis or believe your child may be in crisis, please contact a licensed mental health professional, your primary care provider, or a crisis helpline immediately.

This book is not a crisis intervention tool. It is a starting point.

Abstract

The Whole Child makes a single, evidence-based argument: emotional intelligence is not a trait. It is a skill set. And like every other skill that matters, literacy, critical thinking, resilience, it is built through deliberate practice, consistent modeling, and intentional guidance by the adults in a child's life.

Organized around The Five Roots framework, Notice, Name, Regulate, Connect, Repair, this book provides a complete developmental roadmap for building emotional intelligence from toddlerhood through young adulthood. Each of the twelve chapters addresses one core competency, from emotional vocabulary and self-regulation to empathy, accountability, conflict navigation, boundaries, intrinsic motivation, and digital literacy, with age-specific guidance across five developmental stages: The Builder (Ages 2–5), The Explorer (Ages 6–10), The Questioner (Ages 11–13), The Architect (Ages 14–17), and The Launcher (Ages 18–22).

Drawing on research in neuroscience, developmental psychology, and organizational behavior, and grounded in the author's decades of experience designing emotional intelligence curricula for adult professionals across corporate sectors, *The Whole Child* translates the best of the science into something every parent can use on any Tuesday night.

Emotionally intelligent adults are not born. They are built. This is how.

Table of Contents

ACKNOWLEDGMENTS

Books like this one are written in the margins of a life, in early mornings and late nights, between meetings and obligations, in whatever quiet a person can carve out. The people who make that possible rarely get enough credit.

Izzy, my wife, my person, my favorite human being on the planet, you have the patience of someone who genuinely believes in what the people around her are trying to build. You have watched me disappear into manuscripts more times than either of us can count, and you have never once made me feel guilty for it. You are, in the truest sense, a partner. Everything in this book about showing up consistently, about modeling what you want the people you love to become, about repair and honesty and choosing the harder truer path, I learned much of it from living alongside you.

To everyone who has sat across from me in a conversation about children, parenting, emotional intelligence, or any of the research that found its way into these pages, you are in here, even when I cannot name you personally.

And to the parents reading this: the fact that you are here, taking this seriously, means you are already doing something right. YOUR work matters. Keep going.

INTRODUCTION

Why Emotionally Intelligent Kids Are Rare (And How to Fix That)

Picture this.

It's a Tuesday night. Somewhere in America, pick a suburb, pick a zip code, it doesn't matter, a family is sitting around a dinner table. On paper, everything looks fine. There's food on the table. The kids are doing okay in school. Nobody's in crisis. Dad has a job. Mom has a job. The mortgage is getting paid, mostly on time.

And yet.

Dad hasn't actually asked Mom how she's doing in three weeks, not really, not in the way that requires listening to the answer. Mom is running on empty and has been for months but tells everyone she's fine because she doesn't know how else to be. The fourteen-year-old is scrolling under the table and has said approximately forty words to anyone in the family since last Thursday. The nine-year-old just started crying because his sister looked at him in a way he didn't like, and nobody in the room, including him, has any idea what to do with that.

This is not a family in crisis. This is a Tuesday.

And if you zoom out from that one dinner table to the thousands of dinner tables in that one suburb, to the millions of dinner tables across this country, you see the same essential pattern repeating: people who care about each other deeply, who are genuinely doing their best, who are nonetheless operating without the one set of tools that would make everything, the relationships, the conflicts, the hard days, the inevitable losses, genuinely navigable.

The tools of emotional intelligence.

Now let's do the uncomfortable part.

Look around: not at the kids at those dinner tables, but at the adults. The grown, bill-paying, vote-casting, relationship-having adults who are supposed to have figured this out by now. The ones managing teams at work, navigating marriages, raising children, voting in elections, making decisions that affect other people. What do you actually see?

You see people who cannot have a disagreement without it becoming a war. People who blame everyone around them for problems they created and cannot understand why nothing ever changes. People who fall apart when life gets hard, lash out when they feel threatened, and shut down completely when someone asks them with genuine care how they are doing.

You see people who have never met a feeling they did not either suppress until it exploded, explode at the first available target, or perform dramatically for an audience, turning their own emotional experience into a spectacle rather than a signal.

You see adults who, forty years into their lives, still do not know what to do when they are angry. Still cannot sit with someone else's pain without trying to fix or flee it. Still respond to feedback as though it is a personal attack. Still blame others reflexively because owning their own role in things feels genuinely intolerable.

Here is the thing that should break your heart and then set it on fire with purpose: these are not bad people. Not most of them. Most of them are trying as hard as they know how. Most of them love their families and want good things for their children and lie awake at night wondering why their relationships keep not working the way they hoped.

The problem is not their character. The problem is their toolkit.

Nobody gave them the right tools. Nobody sat down with them, not a parent, not a teacher, not a coach, not anyone, and said with genuine conviction: "Your feelings are real and they matter. Here is what to do with them."

Most of them never heard it.

And so they grew up into adults doing the best they can with tools that were never designed for the job. Hammering screws. Sawing with a butter knife. Wondering why the furniture keeps falling apart.

This book is about making sure your child does not grow up to be one of those adults.

It is about giving them, while you still have the chance and while their foundations are still being built, the complete toolkit.

The Myth of "They'll Figure It Out"

Here is a belief held by a surprising number of otherwise intelligent, otherwise thoughtful parents:

Emotional maturity is something children naturally develop on their own.

Like baby teeth. Like the ability to walk. Like the awkward, lurching progress from dependent infant to mostly-functional adult that seems to happen whether you do anything particularly intentional about it or not. Give it time, give it space, and eventually your kid will figure out how to handle their feelings and relate to other people and navigate the world without leaving a trail of damaged relationships behind them.

This belief is wildly optimistic. It is also completely unsupported by any research that has ever been conducted on the subject.

Emotional intelligence, the ability to identify, understand, manage, and effectively use emotions in yourself and in your interactions with others, is not a personality trait. It does not show up at puberty like acne and existential dread. It does not materialize on some developmental schedule the way object permanence does. It is not hard-wired into human beings the way hunger or the startle reflex is.

It is a skill set.

Emotionally intelligent adults are not born. They are built.

A learnable, teachable, practicable, developable set of skills that grows through intentional experience, consistent modeling, repeated practice, and the kind of guided reflection that requires a thoughtful adult in the picture.

Just like reading. Just like mathematics. Just like playing an instrument or learning to cook or developing the judgment to make good decisions under pressure. All of those things can happen in a rough, accidental way without much deliberate effort, most of us learned to cook by watching someone else and absorbing information osmotically, but they develop far more fully, far more reliably, and far more quickly when someone takes the time to actually teach them.

The difference between EQ and reading is that we have entire institutional systems dedicated to the latter. Schools, curricula, standardized assessments, remediation programs, celebrations of growth and achievement. We have decided, as a society, that literacy is too important to leave to chance, and we have built an infrastructure to ensure it.

Emotional intelligence? We wish the kids well and hope for the best.

And then we wonder, with genuine bewilderment, why our teenagers are emotional wildfires and our adult children cannot hold a job or a relationship for more than two years at a stretch.

Consider what we are actually watching happen. A generation of young adults entering the workforce who are brilliant, genuinely, impressively brilliant, more credentialed than any generation before them, and who nonetheless struggle profoundly with the things that actually determine whether they will thrive: receiving feedback without falling apart, managing conflict without escalating it, persisting through difficulty without requiring constant validation, building and maintaining relationships that require real vulnerability and real accountability.

Corporate managers who have been hiring and developing people for twenty-plus years will tell you, consistently, that technical skills are easy to find. What is rare, genuinely, surprisingly rare, is a person who can hear "here's what you need to work on" and respond with curiosity rather than defensiveness. A person who, when they make a mistake, owns it cleanly and fixes it rather than spending two weeks constructing an elaborate case for why it was actually someone else's fault.

Those people exist. They are extraordinary to work with. And they are extraordinary not because of luck or genetics but because somewhere along the way, someone taught them.

This book is for the people doing the teaching.

This is not a parenting failure, across any individual family, or across our culture broadly. Nobody set out to raise emotionally stunted adults. Nobody decided that teaching feelings was optional or unimportant. We simply did not have a clear, practical, research-grounded guide for how to do it. We inherited our parents' approach, which was inherited from their parents, stretching back through generations in which emotional expression was considered weakness, vulnerability was dangerous, and "I don't know what I'm feeling" was the entire extent of the self-reflection on offer.

It is a knowledge gap. And knowledge gaps are fixable.

That is what you are holding.

What High EQ Actually Predicts

Before we get into how to build it, you deserve to know why it matters this much. Not in the abstract. Concretely, in the specific, measurable, this-is-what-the-research-actually-shows way that should make any parent sit up and take this seriously.

Career success. Daniel Goleman's original synthesis of the emotional intelligence research found that EQ accounted for more of the variance in career success than IQ across virtually every professional domain studied. Technical skills get people hired. Emotional skills determine whether they advance, lead effectively, and sustain high performance over time. The most consistent finding in decades of organizational research: the higher the level of leadership, the more dominant EQ becomes relative to IQ as a predictor of effectiveness. Intelligence gets you in the room. Emotional intelligence determines what happens once you are there.

Relationship stability. John Gottman's longitudinal research at the University of Washington, tracking couples over years and predicting divorce with striking accuracy, identified emotional intelligence as the core differentiating variable between relationships that lasted and those that didn't. Specifically: the ability to regulate during conflict, to repair after rupture, and to maintain genuine empathy for a partner even when you are frustrated with them. These are not personality traits. They are learnable skills. And they are built, or not built, in childhood.

Mental health outcomes. The research on emotional intelligence and mental health is consistent across age groups, cultures, and methodologies: people with higher EQ report lower rates of anxiety and depression, recover more quickly from adversity, and show greater resilience under stress. Marc Brackett's research at Yale found that children with stronger emotional literacy, the ability to identify and name what they are feeling with precision, showed significantly lower rates of behavioral problems, better peer relationships, and better academic outcomes. The emotional vocabulary is not a nicety. It is a protective factor.

Physical health. This one surprises people. Emotional regulation, the ability to manage your own stress response, has direct downstream effects on physical health. Chronically dysregulated stress responses are associated with higher rates of cardiovascular disease, compromised immune function, and accelerated aging at the cellular level. The body keeps score, as Bessel van der Kolk documented extensively. Children who develop robust emotional regulation are not just learning a social skill. They are building physiological resilience that will affect the quality and length of their lives.

Intergenerational transmission. This is perhaps the most consequential finding of all. Adults with high EQ raise children with high EQ. The parenting behaviors that produce emotionally intelligent children, emotional attunement, consistent repair, modeling of regulation, validation of feeling, are themselves products of emotional intelligence. When you build this capacity in yourself and teach it to your children, you are not just changing one person's trajectory. You are changing the default setting for every generation that follows.

Emotionally intelligent adults are not born. They are built.

And the building starts here.

A Brief Note on How We Got Here

For most of human history, emotional management meant suppression. Feel the fear, act anyway, don't talk about it, move on. That was adaptive when survival depended on tight control and a functional exterior. Boys were taught that emotions were obstacles; girls were taught that certain emotions were off the table entirely. Neither approach was malicious. Both made sense in the environments that produced them.

The world changed faster than the instruction manual did. We are raising children for a world where the quality of their lives will be determined not by their ability to suppress and survive, but by their ability to connect authentically, navigate conflict skillfully, and maintain real relationships across decades. The tools most of us were handed do not meet that standard. This book is the update.

What Emotional Intelligence Actually Is

Because "emotional intelligence" has become one of those terms that gets deployed so often it stops meaning anything specific, let's get precise about what we are actually talking about: what we are actually trying to build.

Psychologist Daniel Goleman, whose landmark 1995 book brought the concept into mainstream awareness and whose subsequent research established its practical significance in workplace and personal settings, identified five core components. These are not abstract theoretical constructs, they are observable, measurable capacities that show up in how people behave in real situations.

Self-Awareness

This is the foundation. Knowing what you are feeling, when you are feeling it, and having at least a working theory of why. Sounds elementary, right? It is shockingly rare.

Think about the last time someone asked how you were doing and you actually stopped, checked in with yourself honestly, and gave a real answer rather than "fine." Think about the last time you were in a conflict and, in the middle of it, had clear access to what was actually driving your reaction: not the surface story, not the justified narrative about the other person's behavior, but the real emotional experience underneath.

Self-awareness means having that access. Reliably. Not just in calm retrospect, but in real time, as things are happening.

Most adults have a version of it. Very few have developed it to the degree that makes it genuinely useful under pressure. Because here is the thing about self-awareness: it is easy when nothing is on the line. It becomes the entire game when it is hard.

Self-Regulation

This is the capacity to manage your emotional responses rather than being managed by them. The pause between stimulus and reaction. The space Viktor Frankl wrote about, between what happens to you and what you choose to do about it, where your freedom actually lives.

Self-regulation is not emotional suppression. That distinction matters enormously and we will spend significant time on it in Chapter Four. Suppression buries the feeling. Regulation acknowledges the feeling, gives it its due, and then makes a conscious choice about what to do next.

The person who can say "I am very angry right now and I am choosing to take a walk before I respond" is regulating. The person who denies they are angry while gradually turning into a slow-boiling volcanic situation that eventually erupts all over whoever happens to be nearby on a Thursday afternoon: that is suppression followed by explosion. Most of us know that pattern intimately either from our own experience or from watching the adults around us.

Self-regulation is the skill that makes everything else possible. You cannot access empathy when you are flooded. You cannot problem-solve when you are in survival mode. You cannot have a genuine conversation when your amygdala has taken the wheel. The pause, the capacity to create space between feeling and action, is the master skill.

Motivation

This is the internal dimension, having drives and values that function independently of external reward or punishment. Caring about things because they genuinely matter to you, not because someone is watching, not because there is a prize, not because avoiding failure is the primary engine.

Intrinsic motivation is what makes a person keep working on something after the enthusiasm fades, keep their integrity when no one would know the difference, keep trying in a relationship when it would be easier to leave. It is the fuel that does not run out when the environment stops supplying it.

We live in a moment of extraordinary external motivation, likes, followers, grades, performance reviews, social approval expressed in quantifiable metrics. Children raised almost entirely on that fuel often find, when the external structure disappears, that they have very little idea what they actually care about or why. College students who were brilliant high-achievers in high school sometimes fall apart completely in the absence of external structure, not because they are not smart or capable, but because all their motivation was tethered to something outside themselves, and that tether just snapped.

Building intrinsic motivation is building the internal engine. It is one of the most important long-term investments in this entire book.

Empathy

The ability to accurately perceive and understand what another person is experiencing. Not sympathy, sympathy is feeling sorry for someone, which maintains distance and centers your own emotional response. Empathy is entering into someone else's experience, seeing it from the inside, feeling something of what they feel.

Here is the thing about empathy that gets lost in how it is usually discussed: it is not softness. It is not a niceness skill. It is a precision instrument for understanding other humans, and humans are the primary domain in which we all have to operate.

The leader who cannot accurately read what their team is experiencing makes decisions in an emotional vacuum that consistently miss the mark. The parent who cannot access empathy for their teenager's experience remains perpetually baffled by why the teenager shuts down and stops talking. The partner who cannot imagine what their spouse is feeling remains endlessly surprised by the other person's behavior, as though they are sharing a life with a random stranger rather than a specific person whose inner world is knowable if you pay attention.

Empathy is intelligence applied to people. It is strategic. It is practical. And it is teachable.

Social Skills

The practical application of all the above in actual relationships: which is to say, in the laboratory conditions of real life, with real people, in real time, with real stakes.

Conflict resolution. Communication that lands rather than lands on people. Collaboration. The ability to repair a relationship after a rupture rather than abandoning it. The capacity to give feedback in a way that is actually received. The ability to receive feedback in a way that uses it rather than deflecting it.

These are the skills that make someone genuinely good to be around, genuinely productive to work with, genuinely present in a relationship. They are not personality traits. They are practices, built through intention, modeled by the adults in a child's life, and refined through the accumulated experiences of navigating real human situations with growing skill.

Together, these five components produce a person who is capable of navigating actual life. Not the easy version. Not the one where everything goes well and people are reasonable and nothing requires you to be at your best when you feel your worst. The actual version. The messy, complicated, sometimes beautiful, sometimes brutal version that is waiting for every child we send out into the world.

It means they have the internal resources to find their way back.

That is what we are building. That is the whole point of this book.

Who This Book Is For

This book is for parents. All of them, parents of toddlers who throw spectacular tantrums over the wrong color cup, parents of eight-year-olds who are starting to navigate the complex, sometimes brutal social world of elementary school, parents of teenagers who have apparently forgotten that other humans exist and are regarding the entire family with the kind of weary contempt usually reserved for an unwanted timeshare presentation.

And every exhausted, well-meaning adult in between.

It is also for teachers, particularly the ones who already know that what happens in a classroom is not just academic, that a child who cannot regulate their emotions cannot learn, that the kids who take up the most energy are almost always the kids whose emotional development got disrupted somewhere. It is for school counselors, coaches, mentors, and the aunts and uncles and grandparents who show up consistently and matter enormously even when nobody formally acknowledges their role.

The research on this is consistent: the adults who show up reliably in a child's life all contribute to their emotional development, for better or for worse. It is not a "that's the parents' job" situation. Emotional intelligence is not built by one person in one relationship: it is built across the full range of significant relationships in a child's life, each one offering different experiences, different modeling, different opportunities to practice.

It takes a village. The village needs a handbook. This is it.

What this book is not is another parenting book designed to make you feel like you are doing everything wrong. If you have ever felt, after reading a parenting book, that you were apparently some kind of developmental criminal who had been quietly ruining your child for years without knowing it, I understand, and I am sorry, and this is not that book.

You are here. You are reading. You care enough to invest in this. That already puts you in a completely different category than the millions of parents who are just winging it entirely and hoping for the best. The fact that you are reading this sentence means you are already doing something right.

This is a practical guide. Not a perfect-parenting manual. Not a judgment. A guide, built on research, grounded in clinical reality, and designed for actual human beings navigating actual family life, which includes soccer practice and homework and "what's for dinner" and the days when you lose your temper and say the wrong thing and have to figure out how to repair it.

Every chapter ends with tools you can actually use. Conversations you can actually have. Habits you can actually build into the rhythm of a real life. Because a book full of good ideas that cannot survive contact with a Tuesday is just a comfortable read, and comfort is not what your child needs from you.

The Five Roots: How This Book Is Organized

Before we go any further, let me give you something you can hold onto: a framework that will make everything in this book click into place as you read it.

Emotional intelligence is not one skill. It is a cluster of related capacities that build on each other in a specific sequence. After years of working with the research, the neuroscience, the developmental psychology, the practical parenting literature, I have identified five foundational capacities that every emotionally intelligent person develops. They are not abstract ideals. They are concrete, teachable, practicable skills. And they form the architecture of this entire book.

I call them **The Five Roots.**

Not a ladder. Not a pyramid. Roots: because roots do not develop in a fixed sequence. They grow in response to conditions. They strengthen each other. A child with deep roots can weather almost anything. A child with shallow roots snaps in the first hard wind.

Here they are:

Root One: NOTICE *Feelings are information. Learn to read them.*

The ability to recognize that an emotional state is happening, before being swept away by it. This is the foundation of everything. A child who cannot notice what they are feeling cannot manage it, cannot communicate it, cannot learn from it. Noticing is not the same as wallowing. It is the opposite of being ambushed. It is the skill that makes all other EQ skills possible.

Root Two: NAME *Precision defeats chaos.*

Once a child can notice a feeling, they need the vocabulary to identify it accurately. Not just "mad", but whether they are frustrated, humiliated, resentful, or overwhelmed. Not just "sad", but whether they are disappointed, grieving, lonely, or defeated. This matters neurologically: UCLA neuroscientist Matthew Lieberman's landmark affect labeling research demonstrated that naming an emotion with precision actually reduces the brain's alarm response, measurably decreasing amygdala activation and increasing prefrontal cortex engagement. The right word is not just communication. It is regulation.

Root Three: REGULATE *The pause between impulse and action is where everything important happens.*

This is the capacity to manage emotional activation, to feel something intensely and still choose what to do next. Not suppression. Not explosion. The ability to create space between what is felt and what is done. This is the master skill, the one that makes every other skill accessible. You cannot access empathy when you are flooded. You cannot problem-solve in survival mode. Regulation is the door through which everything else walks.

Root Four: CONNECT *Relationships are the curriculum.*

The ability to understand what another person is experiencing, and to feel genuinely understood in return. Empathy. Safety. Belonging. The capacity to be in a relationship and stay in it across disagreement, disappointment, and distance. This is where emotional intelligence stops being internal and becomes social. Children develop most of their emotional competence in the context of their key relationships, which means connection is not just the goal. It is the vehicle.

Root Five: REPAIR *Mistakes are not the problem. What happens after them is.*

The ability to own errors, make them right, learn from them, and move forward without being defined by them. Accountability without shame. Growth mindset applied to the social and emotional domain. The capacity to rupture a relationship and restore it, to come back together after falling apart. Repair is what makes relationships durable, families honest, and humans resilient.

Every chapter in this book is building one or more of these Five Roots. You will see them labeled at the opening of each chapter so you always know which root you are developing. By the time you reach the end of this book, you will have a complete, integrated system: not a list of tips, not a set of rules, but a living framework you can apply in real time to real situations with your real children.

One more thing about The Five Roots: they are not only for your children.

They are for you, too. As you read, you will recognize yourself in these pages, in the skills that come naturally and in the ones that do not, in the patterns you are already living and in the ones you are still working on. That is not an accident. It is the whole point. Because the parent who is growing in their own Five Roots is simultaneously growing them in their child.

The tree and the roots are the same system.

Let's start planting.

A Note on Tone

Fair warning: this book has a sense of humor.

Parenting is simultaneously the most important and most absurd job on the planet. You are responsible for the complete psychological formation of an entirely new human being. You are building, from raw material, a person who will one day go out into the world and make decisions that affect other people, navigate relationships, raise their own children, and carry forward in some form the legacy of everything you did and did not do.

That is staggering. That is genuinely, weight-of-the-universe staggering.

And half the time you are doing it while operating on four hours of sleep, a gas station coffee, the vague memory of having had a plan for dinner that has long since evaporated, and the dawning awareness that your ten-year-old just tracked something unidentifiable through the hallway you mopped yesterday.

If we cannot laugh at the beautiful, chaotic, frequently ridiculous disaster of raising humans, we will not survive it.

So yes: there will be snark in these pages. There will be honest acknowledgments that children are sometimes absolutely feral, and not in a cute way, and that this is developmentally appropriate but does not make it less exhausting. There will be moments where we say the quiet part loud: the things every parent thinks but mostly keeps to themselves because saying them out loud feels like bad parenting.

There will also be genuine warmth. Because underneath every joke is something I mean completely: this work matters more than almost anything you will ever do. The emotional landscape you help your child build right now, in these years, in these conversations, in these small daily moments that feel insignificant but compound across a childhood, is the ground they will stand on for the rest of their life.

You may not see the returns for years. You may not see them fully until your child is standing in front of their own child and making a choice, a small, barely-visible choice about how to respond to a tantrum or a mistake or a moment of vulnerability, that traces directly back to something you showed them decades ago.

But the returns are coming. The investment is real.

Let's build something worth waiting for.

"The most important thing a parent can do is not to protect their child from difficulty, but to prepare them for it."

HOW TO USE THIS BOOK

This book is organized the way emotional intelligence itself is built, from the inside out.

Part One: The Foundation covers the three things that have to be in place before any specific skill can take root: helping children understand and name their feelings, examining your own role as the primary model, and creating an environment where honesty is genuinely safe. If the foundation is shaky, every chapter after it is harder. If the foundation is solid, every chapter after it compounds.

Part Two: The Core Skills works through the four capacities that form the practical heart of emotional intelligence, self-regulation, empathy, accountability, and learning from mistakes. These are the skills your child will use every day for the rest of their life. They are also the skills most consistently absent in the struggling adults you see around you. Each chapter is self-contained; if you know your child needs specific work in one area, you can go there directly.

Part Three: Advanced EQ covers the territory that emerges as children get older and their world expands, navigating conflict, holding genuine boundaries, developing intrinsic motivation, and operating wisely in the digital world. These chapters build on the core skills and become increasingly relevant from middle childhood through adolescence.

Part Four: The Long Game steps back to the view from ten thousand feet: what you are actually building toward, and how to know when the job is done.

The Five Roots: Your At-a-Glance Map

Each chapter is labeled with the specific Root, or Roots, it develops. Here is your quick reference:

Root	Core Skill	Chapters
NOTICE	Emotional awareness	Ch. 1, Ch. 4, Ch. 10
NAME	Emotional vocabulary and precision	Ch. 1, Ch. 3, Ch. 6
REGULATE	The pause; managing activation	Ch. 4, Ch. 7, Ch. 8, Ch. 9
CONNECT	Empathy, safety, belonging	Ch. 2, Ch. 3, Ch. 5, Ch. 8
REPAIR	Accountability, resilience, growth	Ch. 6, Ch. 7, Ch. 8, Ch. 12

Chapters 11 and 12, and the Conclusion, draw on all five, because digital life and adulthood are where the entire system gets stress-tested.

The Five Developmental Stages: Your Age Guide

Here is the second thing to know before you read a single chapter: **emotional intelligence does not look the same at every age.** The skill is the same. The application is completely different.

Throughout this book, you will find age-band sections woven into each chapter, callout passages that translate the chapter's core concept into what it actually looks like for your specific child, at their specific developmental stage. These are not appendices. They are not optional extras. They are the practical bridge between the principle and your Tuesday night.

Here are the five stages you will encounter:

THE BUILDER (Ages 2–5)

The Builder is in the most formative emotional window of human development. Their brain is being wired for emotional experience right now, in real time, through every interaction with you. They do not yet have the language, the prefrontal cortex development, or the life experience to manage their emotions independently. Everything at this stage is co-regulation first, vocabulary second, and patience always. What you do now does not just teach them: it installs the architecture.

THE EXPLORER (Ages 6–10)

The Explorer has gained enough language, enough self-awareness, and enough cognitive development to start actively learning emotional skills: not just absorbing them. Peers arrive as a powerful new variable. Rules and fairness become intensely important. Identity is forming in relation to others. This is when deliberate instruction starts to compound. The Explorer can have real conversations about feelings, practice real skills, and begin to understand the why behind the what.

THE QUESTIONER (Ages 11–13)

Welcome to the identity crisis. The Questioner is neurologically reorganizing: the brain is literally undergoing a second wave of major development, and the prefrontal cortex is once again temporarily offline in ways that feel, from the outside, like regression. Peer approval now outranks parental approval as the primary social currency. Abstract thinking is newly available but wildly inconsistent. The key at this stage is not control. It is relationship maintenance. You are keeping the connection alive through the turbulence so the runway is intact when they are ready to land.

THE ARCHITECT (Ages 14–17)

The Architect is actively building their adult identity, testing values against reality, pushing against authority to find the edges of their own personhood, taking risks because the developing brain literally seeks novelty as part of healthy adolescent programming. None of this is malfunction. All of it is development. Your role shifts from instructor to consultant. The skills you installed in the Builder and Explorer years are now being tested under live fire. The goal is to stay in relationship, hold the boundaries that matter, and trust the roots you planted.

THE LAUNCHER (Ages 18–22)

The Launcher is the first-year field test. Everything that was abstract, accountability, empathy, regulation, repair, is now being applied in dorm rooms, first jobs, serious relationships, and adult-scale consequences. The prefrontal cortex is still finishing construction. The emotional patterns installed across childhood are now running largely without parental support or supervision. This is the stage that reveals what the roots actually look like, and the stage where it is still entirely possible to deepen them, if the relationship between parent and young adult remains genuine.

A few notes on how to read this:

You do not have to read it in order, though the progression has logic. If your child is nine and you are in the middle of a specific storm, accountability resistance, say, or social conflict, go directly to the relevant chapter. The tools sections at the end of each chapter are designed to be usable without reading everything that came before.

The tools are real. Use them. They are not theoretical exercises or idealized conversation scripts that could only happen in a calm controlled environment. They are things you can actually do on a Wednesday, with your actual children, in your actual life. Start with one. See what happens. Add another.

Every chapter references research and named researchers. The bibliography in the back will take you deeper if you want it. But this is not an academic text, and you do not need to read a single additional source to implement everything in this book. The research is here to show you why the practices work, not to make you feel like you need a PhD before you can start.

Finally: this book will ask you to look at yourself. Not with judgment, with curiosity. The most important variable in your child's emotional development is not a curriculum or a technique. It is you, specifically, your own emotional patterns, your own history, and what you are modeling in the thousands of small moments that make up a childhood.

That is not a comfortable thing to sit with. It is also the most empowering thing in this entire book. Because it means that every time you regulate when you wanted to react, every time you repair after you got it wrong, every time you choose honesty over comfort or curiosity over judgment, you are doing the work. In real time. With real effect.

You are always teaching. The only question is what.

PART ONE: THE FOUNDATION

CHAPTER ONE

Feelings Are Data, Not Drama

The Five Roots this chapter develops: **NOTICE · NAME**

Something nobody tells you about emotions, probably because it sounds too clinical for a topic this personal:

Feelings are neurological events.

Not metaphors. Not performances. Not character flaws or signs of weakness or evidence that something has gone wrong in your child's development. Actual, physical, electrochemical events occurring in an actual brain that is doing exactly what brains are designed to do when they perceive something that matters.

When your seven-year-old melts down because you cut her sandwich into triangles instead of rectangles, something real is happening in her brain. Neurotransmitters are firing. The amygdala, the brain's alarm system, the structure responsible for detecting threat and initiating the stress response, has been activated. Cortisol and adrenaline are coursing through a nervous system that is, by the way, still literally under construction and will not be fully built until her mid-twenties.

This is not drama. This is biology.

Now, that does not mean every emotional response is proportional, appropriate, or something you are obligated to indulge. A meltdown over sandwich geometry is not a crisis that requires therapy or a reevaluation of your parenting. It is a small child encountering the gap between what she expected and what happened, and responding with the full-body emotional reaction that is the only tool she currently has for that situation.

But here is the part worth taking seriously: it is real. The distress she is experiencing, as spectacularly out of proportion as it appears, is a genuine neurological state. And the way you respond to it, the way you respond to all the emotional expressions from your children across all the years you have them, shapes how they relate to their own inner life for decades.

Not just this moment. Decades.

Every response you give to your child's emotional experience is a small lesson in one of two things: either emotions are manageable, nameable, and safe to have, or they are dangerous, shameful, and best suppressed or performed rather than actually felt. Those lessons accumulate. They become the architecture of an inner life.

That architecture is what we are building in this chapter.

A father named Marcus told me about the moment he understood this. His eight-year-old daughter, Nia, had burst into tears at dinner because her best friend had been assigned a different classroom for the new school year. "She'll still be your friend," he started to say, and then stopped himself. He had read something about this, somewhere. Instead, he put down his fork and said, "That is really disappointing. You were counting on being together." Nia looked up at him. "Yeah," she said. Then, after a moment: "It's actually kind of scary too." He hadn't expected that word. He said, "Tell me about the scary part." And she did. Twenty minutes later she had talked herself into a plan, she would ask if they could eat lunch together. She solved it herself. He had done nothing but name what she was feeling and make room for more. He told me it was the first time he realized that solving the problem had never been the point.

A Quick Tour of the Emotional Brain

Before we talk about what to do with emotions, it helps to understand what is actually happening in the brain when they show up. Not in a neuroscience-lecture way, but in the practical way that actually changes how you respond in the moment.

The human brain, for all its extraordinary complexity, operates in a rough hierarchy. At the base is the brainstem, the ancient, automatic part that handles breathing, heart rate, and the basic survival functions you do not have to think about. Above that, the limbic system, including the amygdala, handles emotional processing, threat detection, and the social signals that have always mattered enormously for survival. At the top, the prefrontal cortex handles reasoning, planning, perspective-taking, impulse control, and all the things we think of as sophisticated human judgment.

These systems communicate constantly, but they do not have equal authority under all conditions.

When the amygdala detects threat, real or perceived, physical or emotional, it can essentially commandeer the entire system. This is what researchers call the "amygdala hijack," a term coined by Daniel Goleman. The thinking brain goes partially offline. The survival brain takes the wheel. Rational conversation, perspective-taking, problem-solving, empathy, all those prefrontal cortex functions become dramatically less available.

This is why you cannot reason your child out of a meltdown while they are in the middle of one. It is not stubbornness. It is not manipulation. It is a brain in survival mode, doing exactly what it evolved to do, without the regulatory capacity to override it because that capacity is still being built.

Here is the part that is both sobering and important: the prefrontal cortex, the seat of all those sophisticated emotional regulation functions, does not fully mature until the mid-twenties. The regulatory hardware is literally incomplete. We are asking children to regulate emotions with equipment that is not yet fully operational, and then expressing bewilderment when they cannot do it consistently.

This does not mean children cannot develop emotional regulation skills. They absolutely can, and the development of those skills is the entire project of this book. But it means that realistic expectations, patient repetition, and understanding the actual biology are all essential prerequisites.

ROOT ONE, NOTICE: What This Looks Like At Each Stage

THE BUILDER (Ages 2–5): The Builder does not yet have the cognitive architecture to notice their own emotional states, they are entirely inside the feeling, with no vantage point from which to observe it. Your job is to do the noticing for them. When you see the flushed face, the clenched fists, the sudden stillness before the storm: name what you see out loud. "You look really frustrated right now." "I can see something scared you." You are not asking them to agree. You are teaching them that feelings have names by modeling the practice of naming them. Over thousands of repetitions, that external narration becomes an internal voice.

THE EXPLORER (Ages 6–10): The Explorer has enough self-awareness to start noticing their emotional states in real time, with support. They can often tell you something is wrong before they can tell you what. "I feel weird" is a complete and honest answer from an eight-year-old, and it is progress. Work with it: "Where do you feel the weird? What does it feel like?" They are building the observational habit. Your role shifts from narrator to curious guide.

THE QUESTIONER (Ages 11–13): The Questioner can notice feelings but may be intensely reluctant to admit it, particularly to you. Peer culture begins to treat emotional expression as vulnerability, and vulnerability is dangerous at this stage. Do not force it. Instead, make noticing safe by noticing your own feelings out loud without drama. "I noticed I felt kind of anxious before that meeting today." Normalize the practice without targeting them. They are watching. When they see noticing as something competent adults do rather than something weakness requires, the resistance usually softens.

THE ARCHITECT (Ages 14–17): The Architect has the cognitive capacity to notice their emotional states with real sophistication: but the adolescent nervous system is running hot, and the gap between noticing and acting on what they notice is still narrow. They feel everything at high volume. What helps at this stage is not instruction but invitation: "What was going on for you in there?" rather than "Why did you react like that?" The first invites self-reflection. The second triggers defense.

THE LAUNCHER (Ages 18–22): The Launcher is applying NOTICE in adult contexts, the workplace conflict, the relationship rupture, the moment before a decision that matters. Check in as a peer, not a parent: "How are you actually doing?" The emotional awareness you built in the earlier stages is now operating largely without you. What they still benefit from is the knowledge that noticing and naming are practices the adults in their life continue to do, not something they graduated out of.

The Vocabulary Problem

Ask most children how they are feeling and you will get one of three answers: good, bad, or fine.

Fine, as any parent knows, is the universal signal that something is definitely wrong and no further information will be forthcoming.

Fine is emotional armor. Fine is a monosyllabic drawbridge pulled firmly up against inquiry.

This is not because children do not have feelings. They are swimming in feelings essentially all the time: an almost continuous stream of emotional experience that most adults have learned to partially filter out but that children are still living in fully, without the buffer that comes from years of practice with emotional regulation.

The problem is not the absence of feeling. It is the absence of vocabulary.

And vocabulary, it turns out, matters enormously: not just for communication, but for the actual neurological experience of emotion itself.

Research by neuroscientist Matthew Lieberman and his colleagues at UCLA found something remarkable: the simple act of labeling an emotion, putting words to what you are feeling, measurably reduces activity in the amygdala and increases activity in the prefrontal cortex. The thinking brain comes back online. The alarm system quiets down. Naming a feeling literally, measurably, neurologically calms the brain.

This is why every good therapist asks "how does that make you feel?" It is not a cliché. It is a clinical intervention based on how the brain actually works. The question forces the prefrontal cortex to engage with the emotional experience, and that engagement itself is regulating.

For children, who are in the early stages of developing both vocabulary and the self-reflective habit of applying that vocabulary to their own experience, this is not a minor thing. It is foundational.

Children who develop a rich emotional vocabulary, who can distinguish between frustrated and furious, between disappointed and devastated, between nervous and terrified, between embarrassed and ashamed, show measurably better outcomes across virtually every domain that matters: peer relationships, conflict resolution, academic performance, and long-term mental health. Marc Brackett's research at the Yale Center for Emotional Intelligence, spanning over two decades and tens of thousands of students, documents this relationship consistently across age groups, income levels, and cultures.

Words give children power over their inner experience. Without the words, the feelings are just weather, powerful, unpredictable forces that arrive and depart and cannot be influenced or understood. With the words, the feelings become information. Manageable. Discussable. Something to work with rather than be worked over by.

ROOT TWO, NAME: Building Emotional Vocabulary At Each Stage

THE BUILDER (Ages 2–5): Start with three to five big, clear words. Mad. Sad. Scared. Happy. Excited. Do not push for nuance yet: the goal right now is simply to establish that feelings have names at all. Use the words constantly in your running narration: "You're so happy right now!" "That scared you, didn't it?" Read books with big emotional moments and pause to name what the character is feeling. The vocabulary installs through repetition, not instruction.

THE EXPLORER (Ages 6–10): This is the prime window for vocabulary expansion. The Explorer is developmentally ready to move beyond the basics and genuinely curious about precision. Introduce the feelings wheel. Play the "more specific" game: "You said you're mad, but are you frustrated, jealous, or embarrassed? What's the closest one?" This is not pedantry. It is building the emotional GPS that will guide them for life. When they get the right word and it lands, when they say "I'm not mad, I'm disappointed" and you can see it click: that is one of the most satisfying moments in parenting an Explorer.

THE QUESTIONER (Ages 11–13): Do not let the social cool-down of early adolescence fool you into thinking the vocabulary work is done. The Questioner is encountering more complex emotions than they have ever faced, social exclusion, romantic longing, the specific grief of realizing a friend has changed, the complicated mixture of pride and terror when they do something genuinely brave. They need more words now, not fewer. Feed the vocabulary through conversations about characters in books, movies, or situations that happened to someone else. "What do you think he was actually feeling in that scene?" is a much easier question to answer than "What are you feeling right now?"

THE ARCHITECT (Ages 14–17): The Architect's emotional life is rich, complex, and often private. Vocabulary work at this stage is less about direct instruction and more about modeling. Use precise emotional language yourself: "I was embarrassed, not actually angry." "That left me feeling genuinely proud of myself." When you use specific words for your own experience without making it a lesson, you are still expanding their working vocabulary. They will find themselves reaching for those words when they need them.

THE LAUNCHER (Ages 18–22): Emotional vocabulary in the Launcher years becomes a professional and relational asset: the young adult who can accurately say "I felt undermined, not just criticized" in a difficult conversation at work is operating at a level that gets noticed. Your role now is to affirm, not teach: when they use precise emotional language with you, meet it in kind. The conversation between parent and Launcher is its own modeling moment.

Beyond Mad, Sad, and Happy

The average emotional vocabulary that children are explicitly taught contains roughly six words, corresponding to the six basic emotions identified by psychologist Paul Ekman as universal across human cultures: happiness, sadness, anger, fear, surprise, and disgust.

These six are a fine starting point. They are not nearly sufficient for an actual human life.

Consider the difference between being angry and being humiliated. Both involve activation, both might look similar from the outside, raised voice, tense body, flushed face, but they are fundamentally different experiences that call for completely different responses and have completely different implications for what the person needs.

A child who can only say "I'm mad" when they are actually experiencing humiliation has no access to the underlying truth of their situation. They cannot communicate what they actually need. The adult trying to help them cannot identify what actually happened. The intervention, however well-intentioned, misses the target entirely because the emotional GPS has no coordinates.

Now multiply that across the entire range of human emotional experience:

There is a world of difference between being sad and grieving, between the passing sadness of a disappointment and the deep, body-heavy grief of a real loss. Between being nervous and being anxious, between the excitement-adjacent flutter before something new and the dread that comes from anticipating something genuinely threatening. Between feeling happy and feeling proud, between the pleasant affect of a good day and the specific, earned satisfaction of having done something that matters and done it well.

Each distinction points to something different happening in the person's experience. Each requires a different response. Each opens a different conversation.

The psychologist Lisa Feldman Barrett, whose research on emotion has significantly updated our understanding of how feelings are actually constructed in the brain, argues that emotional granularity, the ability to make fine-grained distinctions between emotional states, is one of the most significant factors in emotional wellbeing. People with high emotional granularity are better at regulating their emotions, make better decisions under pressure, use coping strategies more flexibly, and are less likely to engage in self-destructive behaviors when distressed.

Emotional granularity is, essentially, the product of emotional vocabulary. You cannot experience the distinction between humiliated and angry if you only have one word for both of them.

The tool most commonly recommended for building this vocabulary, and it works remarkably well, even with adults who are encountering it for the first time, is the feelings wheel. Originally developed by therapist Gloria Wilcox and subsequently refined in numerous iterations, the feelings wheel organizes emotions in concentric rings from basic to nuanced. At the center are the core states: joy, sadness, anger, fear, disgust, surprise. Moving outward, each basic emotion branches into increasingly specific variations.

Anger, for example, might branch into frustrated, irritated, jealous, resentful, betrayed, humiliated. Sadness might branch into lonely, disappointed, devastated, grieving, regretful, isolated.

Using the feelings wheel with children, even young children, who can work with simplified versions, does two things simultaneously. It expands their vocabulary in a concrete, visual way. And it models the practice of emotional self-examination: looking inward, identifying what is happening, reaching for precision rather than settling for the first word that comes.

That practice, modeled and repeated across years, becomes automatic. The child who learns to ask "what exactly am I feeling?" becomes the adult who actually knows.

Where Do You Feel It in Your Body?

Here is a question that works especially well with younger children, and also with older children and adults who have learned to live primarily in their heads and have lost touch with the bodily dimension of emotional experience:

"Where do you feel it in your body?"

Emotions are not abstract. They have physical signatures, consistent, recognizable patterns of sensation that show up in the body before they register cognitively. Anxiety tends to live in the chest and the stomach: the tightness across the sternum, the low-grade nausea, the shallow breathing. Anger often manifests as heat in the face, tension in the jaw and shoulders, a tightening in the fists. Sadness can feel like heaviness in the chest, a constriction in the throat, a particular kind of fatigue that is different from being tired. Excitement and anxiety, interestingly, feel almost identical in the body, which is why reframing nervous energy as excitement is actually a neurologically coherent strategy, not just a motivational poster.

When a child cannot find the words for what they are feeling, when "fine" is all that is available, or when they genuinely do not know, the body often knows before the mind does.

"You look like something is bothering you. Where do you feel it?" is a question that many children who cannot answer "how are you feeling?" can answer with surprising specificity. "In my chest." "My tummy feels weird." "My throat feels tight." Once they have located the physical sensation, the emotional label often follows naturally. The brain, given a somatic clue, can often find its way to the word.

This approach is grounded in what clinicians call interoception: the ability to sense and interpret signals from inside the body. Sarah Garfinkel's research at the University of Sussex and related work by Hugo Critchley have consistently shown that well-developed interoceptive awareness is associated with better emotional regulation, better mental health outcomes, and even better physical health. People who can accurately read their own internal states catch emotional activation earlier, before it escalates into something harder to manage. They notice the first signs of anxiety before it becomes panic. They feel the beginning of anger before it becomes rage.

Teaching children to notice the body is teaching them to catch the warning signs early. It is building the early detection system that makes regulation possible before the alarm goes fully off.

This is not yoga philosophy. This is neuroscience with immediate practical application.

NOTICE + NAME: Body Awareness At Each Stage

THE BUILDER (Ages 2–5): Body awareness at this stage is entirely concrete and physical. Name the sensations you observe: "Your fists are tight. That means your body is really upset right now." Touch is co-regulating: a hand on the shoulder, a slow breath modeled together, a hug offered (not demanded). You are building the connection between internal sensation and external word from the outside in. Eventually it becomes theirs.

THE EXPLORER (Ages 6–10): The Explorer can absolutely learn to locate feelings in their body, and most of them find it fascinating, because children this age are intensely curious about how things work, including themselves. "Show me where you feel nervous in your body. Is it in your tummy? Your chest? Your throat?" Make a body map together, draw a simple outline and let them mark where each emotion lives in their particular body. It becomes a reference document and a shared language.

THE QUESTIONER (Ages 11–13): Adolescence brings a complicated new relationship with the body, and body-based emotional work at this stage requires sensitivity. The Questioner's body is changing and often feels unfamiliar and uncomfortable. Frame body awareness in terms they find practical rather than therapeutic: "When you're about to explode at someone, what does it feel like right before? What's the signal?" Putting it in functional terms, this is information that helps you catch things early, is more accessible than asking them to explore their feelings, which can feel exposing.

THE ARCHITECT (Ages 14–17): The Architect often notices their body-emotion connection in retrospect: "I didn't realize I was anxious until after." This is developmentally normal and also something you can gently work with: "What would have been the earlier signal, if you'd been watching for it?" Building the early detection system, the moment before the escalation rather than the escalation itself, is the most valuable body awareness work at this stage. It is also the same skill that will serve them in every high-stakes adult situation they encounter.

THE LAUNCHER (Ages 18–22): For the Launcher, body-emotion awareness is a stress management and performance tool, not just a feelings tool. Frame it as such. Athletes use it. Executives use it. The ability to notice "I'm running hot right now and should not send that email" is worth more in the first year of a job than almost any technical skill. If you can have that conversation without it feeling like a parenting lecture, you are giving them something genuinely useful.

The Validation Rule

Before we go any further, there is one principle so fundamental to emotional intelligence development that everything else in this book depends on it. It is the rule beneath all the other rules. The practice that makes all the other practices possible.

Validate the feeling before you do anything else.

Not the behavior. Not necessarily the interpretation. Not the child's version of events. The feeling.

When a child is in emotional distress, when they are crying, or raging, or shut down, or overwhelmed, their brain is in what neuroscientists call an emotionally flooded state. The prefrontal cortex, the part of the brain that handles language, rational thought, perspective-taking, and problem-solving, is functioning at dramatically reduced capacity. The amygdala has the wheel.

You cannot reason with a flooded brain. You cannot teach it, redirect it, problem-solve with it, or effectively consequence it. Not right now. Not while it is flooded.

What you can do is help regulate it. And the single most powerful co-regulating tool available to a parent, more powerful than distraction, more powerful than removal, more powerful than any behavioral intervention, is simple, consistent emotional validation.

"I can see you are really upset right now. That makes sense."

That is it. That is the whole move. Eight words, or some version of them, adapted to the moment and the child and the situation. But the structure is always the same: I see what you are feeling. It is real. It is okay to have it. You are not alone in it.

What this communicates to the child, in a way that bypasses the flooded prefrontal cortex and goes directly to the alarm-sounding amygdala, is profoundly regulating: you are seen, you are safe, this feeling is survivable, and the person you depend on is not frightened or overwhelmed by what you are experiencing.

That message, received repeatedly across years, builds something researchers call emotional security, the deep, embodied understanding that your inner experience is real and does not have to be hidden, that feelings are manageable rather than dangerous, that you will not be abandoned or punished for having them. John Bowlby's foundational attachment theory, extended through Mary Ainsworth's Strange Situation research and decades of subsequent work, established that this felt sense of security is not a soft outcome, it is one of the most powerful predictors of psychological health across the entire lifespan.

Emotionally secure children are not just happier. They are measurably more resilient, more empathetic, more able to regulate themselves because they have internalized, through thousands of small validating interactions, the understanding that emotions are survivable. They got that understanding from you.

The validation always comes first. Before the lesson. Before the redirect. Before the consequence. Before the problem-solving.

The feeling gets acknowledged. Then everything else.

What Not to Say (And Why It Matters More Than You Think)

With the absolute best of intentions, parents regularly say things to their children that teach them to distrust or suppress their own emotional experience. These phrases are so culturally embedded that many of them feel not just normal but virtuous, like responsible parenting, like toughening up a child for a world that is not going to be gentle with them.

Understanding why they are actually counterproductive, and what they teach children to believe about their inner lives, changes them from bad habits to something you simply stop doing, because once you see it you cannot unsee it.

"You're fine."

The child is clearly not fine. The message delivered, usually with good intentions, usually to interrupt an escalating emotional response before it gets bigger, is: your perception of your own inner state is incorrect. I can see from the outside that you are fine, and your internal experience of distress is wrong.

This is deeply disorienting for a child who is learning to read their own signals. They are experiencing something real and being told it is not real. Over time, they learn to override their own internal experience, to discount their own signals, to perform "fine" as a way of navigating a world that does not believe their experience. They become adults who literally do not know what they are feeling because they trained themselves out of noticing.

"Don't cry."

Crying is the body's natural neurological reset mechanism. Crying releases cortisol and other stress hormones. Crying activates the parasympathetic nervous system, the body's rest-and-digest counterpart to the fight-or-flight response. Crying, in other words, is not the problem: it is the solution the body is already deploying.

Suppressing it does not eliminate the emotional experience. It interrupts the body's own regulation process and drives the unprocessed distress elsewhere, usually into the nervous system in ways that compound over time.

Boys in particular receive this message with extraordinary consistency from an extraordinarily early age. The cost is decades of emotional suppression, an inability to access vulnerability, and a nervous system that has been trained to express distress as anger because anger was the only feeling that was allowed. An enormous amount of male rage in adult life is suppressed sadness, grief, and hurt that was told, for thirty or forty years, not to exist.

"You're being so sensitive."

Said as a criticism, which it almost always is, this tells a child that their emotional responsiveness is a character flaw. That feeling things deeply is something to be ashamed of and corrected.

High sensitivity is not a disorder. It is a trait, present in roughly fifteen to twenty percent of the population according to psychologist Elaine Aron's research, that correlates with deep empathy, rich inner life, strong aesthetic responsiveness, and profound creativity. Many of the most exceptional artists, therapists, teachers, and leaders are highly sensitive people who learned to use their sensitivity as an asset rather than suppress it as a liability.

The child who is told repeatedly that their sensitivity is a problem often grows into an adult who is cut off from their greatest strength. Telling them that their capacity to feel deeply is embarrassing is like telling a gifted athlete that their coordination is a character flaw.

"It's not a big deal."

The ability to assess the proportionality of your emotional response is a developmental skill that takes years to build. It requires a developed prefrontal cortex and a library of experiences against which to compare the current situation. Seven-year-olds do not have that library. Neither do many teenagers. Proportionality comes with time, experience, and modeling.

When you tell a child that what they are experiencing "is not a big deal," you are not teaching proportionality. You are teaching them that when they bring their distress to you, they will receive a dismissal. They adjust accordingly: they stop bringing their distress to you. This seems to solve the problem in the short term. It creates a much more significant problem in the medium and long term, when they are a teenager with real problems and they have learned from years of experience that you are not the person to bring them to.

"Calm down."

Has any human being, in the entire recorded history of human interaction, ever calmed down because someone told them to calm down? Not once. Because "calm down" is a destination announcement with no directions: it tells you where to go and provides absolutely no mechanism for getting there.

When you tell a child to calm down, you are expressing your own need for the distressing behavior to stop without providing any tools for stopping it. The child is not failing to comply out of defiance. They do not know how to calm down yet. That is why you are here.

Instead of "calm down," try: "Let's take a breath together." This is different in two important ways. It offers a concrete strategy. And it makes you a companion in the regulation rather than an authority demanding a result.

The Check-In Habit

One of the most consistently effective tools for building emotional vocabulary and self-awareness over time requires nothing more than a few minutes and a genuine question.

The daily check-in.

Not a formal interrogation. Not a structured emotional processing session. Just a habit woven into existing routines, dinner, car rides, the ten minutes before bed, where emotional awareness is invited and normalized as part of the rhythm of family life.

The questions do not need to be elaborate:

"What was the hardest part of today?"

"Did anything bother you that you haven't had a chance to talk about yet?"

"What feeling showed up the most for you today?"

"If today was a weather report, what would it be?"

That last one works particularly well with younger children who may not yet have the vocabulary for direct emotional inquiry but can readily imagine whether their day felt like sunshine, a thunderstorm, partly cloudy with a chance of good things, or a tornado.

The goal of the check-in is not to extract information or solve problems. It is to establish a norm, to make emotional awareness and communication a standard feature of family life rather than something that only happens in crisis. The implicit message is this: in our family, we pay attention to our inner lives. We talk about what we feel. That is normal here. There is nothing unusual or alarming about having feelings and naming them.

That norm, practiced daily across years of childhood, becomes internalized. The child who grows up in a home where emotional check-ins are the default becomes the teenager who actually talks to their parents: not because they have been required to, but because it never occurred to them not to. The emotional channel is open because it has always been open.

And here is something worth noting: the check-in works best when it goes both ways. When you share your own emotional experience, briefly, authentically, in age-appropriate terms, the child receives something beyond information. They receive the message that having and expressing feelings is something adults do too. That it is not a childhood phase you grow out of. That the emotional life of the family includes everyone.

That is a lesson that lands.

NOTICE + NAME: The Check-In At Each Stage

THE BUILDER (Ages 2–5): Formal check-ins do not work yet, Builders live in the present moment and do not have the reflective capacity to review their emotional day. What works instead is real-time naming woven into your routines. At bath time, bedtime, in the car: "You seemed really happy at the park today." "You got frustrated when we had to leave, that's hard." You are doing the check-in for them, showing them what it looks like, installing the habit before they can run it independently.

THE EXPLORER (Ages 6–10): This is the golden window for the check-in habit. The Explorer is old enough to reflect, young enough to still find it genuinely fun, and not yet self-conscious about it. The weather report question works beautifully at this age, "If your day was weather, what would it be?" Open-ended, low-stakes, and surprisingly revealing. Establish it as a dinner table ritual now, while they still want to participate, and you are building a channel that may stay open through the harder years ahead.

THE QUESTIONER (Ages 11–13): The Questioner may begin to resist the check-in they happily participated in as an Explorer. Do not abandon it, adapt it. Keep it lighter. Make it a two-way exchange where you share something real first, without requiring reciprocation. "I had a frustrating day, my thing fell apart at the last minute. How about you?" Sometimes they will deflect. Sometimes they will surprise you entirely. The goal is to keep the channel technically open even when they are not using it, because the day will come when they need it badly and they will only use it if it has never fully closed.

THE ARCHITECT (Ages 14–17): Do not force it. The Architect who feels interrogated shuts down faster than any developmental stage. Shift from scheduled check-ins to casual ambient connection, the car ride, the late-night kitchen encounter, the side-by-side moments that do not feel like emotional processing sessions. "How are you doing with everything?" delivered casually, without expectation, while doing something else, often gets more truth than a formal sit-down. The check-in at this stage is less a habit and more a posture, being available without being demanding.

THE LAUNCHER (Ages 18–22): The check-in with a Launcher is a peer conversation. They are no longer reporting to you; they are choosing to confide in you, and that choice deserves to be honored with genuine curiosity and without unsolicited advice. "How are you actually doing?", and then listening without fixing, is one of the most important things you can do to stay in real relationship with a young adult. The parents who remain genuinely close to their Launchers are almost always the ones who learned to receive rather than direct.

The Takeaway

Feelings are not problems to be solved, performances to be managed, or signs that something has gone wrong. They are information, rich, specific, sometimes uncomfortable data about what a person needs, values, fears, and loves.

Teaching children to receive that data with curiosity rather than panic, to name it with precision rather than bury it in vague discomfort, and to use it as a guide rather than a tyrant: that is the first and most foundational gift of emotional intelligence.

Everything else in this book sits on top of this foundation: the radical, simple, endlessly powerful idea that your child's feelings are real, their feelings are useful, and their feelings deserve your attention.

Not just your management. Your attention.

Your child's emotional life is not an inconvenience. It is not a phase. It is not something to toughen them out of.

It is the whole point.

Emotionally intelligent adults are not born. They are built, in the small moments, by the adults paying attention. This is Chapter One of that building.

In Chapter Two, we turn to the most powerful, and most uncomfortable, truth in this entire book: before you can teach emotional intelligence, you have to model it. Which means we start with you.

TOOLS FOR CHAPTER ONE

The Feelings Wheel Check-In Print or draw a feelings wheel, you can find free versions easily online, or draw a simplified version with concentric circles. Once a week at dinner, each family member picks a word from the outer ring that describes something they felt that day. No explanation required unless they want to share. The goal is normalizing emotional vocabulary for the entire family, including parents. When children watch adults name their feelings casually and without drama, it becomes the most normal thing in the world.

The Body Scan Question When a child seems upset but cannot articulate why, when "fine" is all that is available, try: "Close your eyes for a second. Where in your body do you feel something right now?" Once they locate it, you can follow up: "If that feeling had a color, what color would it be? If it had a shape, what shape?" This creative, sensory approach often unlocks language that direct emotional questioning cannot reach. It works because it bypasses the cognitive demand of naming an emotion and asks instead for something more immediately accessible: a physical sensation. The emotional label usually follows.

The Validation Formula Before any redirect, lesson, or problem-solving, practice this sequence until it is automatic: "I can see you are [feeling]. That makes sense because [reason]. I am here." Three components: acknowledgment of the feeling, validation of the reason, and presence. It takes fifteen seconds. It changes the emotional climate of an interaction completely. Practice it in low-stakes moments so it is available in high-stakes ones. Write it on a sticky note on the refrigerator if it helps.

The Emotions Dictionary Start a running list, physical or digital, whatever works for your family, of emotion words your household discovers and uses. Let the children add to it. Make it a game: who can find the most specific word for what they are feeling? The family with the biggest feelings vocabulary wins at emotional intelligence, and they have fun building it.

The Two-Way Check-In Establish a brief daily check-in, before dinner, at bedtime, in the car, where everyone gets to share one thing about the emotional texture of their day. The critical element: parents go too. Not with drama or oversharing, just briefly and honestly. "I felt frustrated at work today because a project I worked hard on got changed at the last minute. I was proud of how I handled it though." Model the vocabulary, model the normalcy, model the self-reflection. The children are watching and learning what emotional engagement looks like from someone who is already on the other side of childhood.

CHAPTER TWO

You Are the Blueprint

The Five Roots this chapter develops: **CONNECT**

—, and if you are a parent, it has either already happened or it is coming for you like a freight train, where you watch your child do something and think, with a mixture of pride and low-grade horror: that is exactly what I do.

Maybe it is the way they tilt their head when they are thinking through a problem, the precise angle you have seen in photographs of yourself going back to childhood. Maybe it is their laugh, your laugh, coming out of a smaller face. Maybe it is something more uncomfortable: the way they deflect a compliment with a self-deprecating joke, the way they shut down completely when they feel overwhelmed instead of asking for help, the way they snap when they are stressed and take it out on whoever happens to be standing nearest to them.

The way they do that thing you do. The thing you have been trying to stop doing for years.

Children are watching us with the focused, unrelenting attention of a documentary filmmaker who has complete access, no editorial filter, an unlimited budget, and the specific intention of figuring out how humans work by studying the ones closest to them. They are capturing everything. The way we speak to our partners when we think the kids are not listening. The way we handle disappointment when we thought we were handling it privately. The way we talk about people we disagree with, how much patience we extend to strangers versus the people we love most, the words we reach for when we are hurt, the behaviors we deploy when we are scared.

And then, because this is how humans are designed to learn, they replicate it.

Not as a choice. Not as defiance. As acquisition: the same deeply wired process that taught them to walk, to talk, to navigate social situations, to understand what it means to be a person in the world. We are their first and most powerful model of personhood. We are the template from which they are building.

This is simultaneously the most humbling and most motivating truth in all of parenting. You are the most powerful emotional education your child will ever receive. Not the parenting books you read. Not the school counselor or the soccer coach or the children's therapist, however good they are. Not the carefully worded conversations you have about feelings and values on Sunday mornings when everyone is calm and reasonable.

You. What you actually do, in the actual moments, when you are not thinking about it and the cameras are rolling anyway.

The Science of Watching and Learning

Albert Bandura was a psychologist at Stanford who spent decades studying how humans learn from observing other humans, and his findings, consolidated under the umbrella of social learning theory, have been among the most replicated and practically significant in all of developmental psychology.

The core finding is simple and somewhat unsettling: children do not primarily learn behavior from what they are told. They learn it from what they watch.

Bandura's famous Bobo doll experiments in the early 1960s demonstrated this with striking clarity. Children who watched an adult behave aggressively toward an inflatable doll subsequently imitated that aggression, spontaneously, creatively, with variations of their own, at dramatically higher rates than children who had not observed the aggressive model. The children who watched a non-aggressive adult showed dramatically lower aggression. The behavior transferred through observation with startling efficiency.

What was true for aggression toward a Bobo doll is true for every other behavior, emotional and otherwise, that children watch the adults in their lives perform. Emotional suppression. Conflict escalation. Accountability and repair. The management of disappointment. The response to criticism. The way we treat people who have less power than we do. The way we talk about ourselves.

Children are learning all of it, all the time, from watching us. The lesson is delivered whether or not we intend to teach it.

Here is the uncomfortable part of this, stated as plainly as it deserves to be stated:

You cannot lecture your child into emotional health while modeling emotional dysfunction. It does not work. The behavior they observe does not just compete with the lesson you deliver: it overwrites it. Completely. Every time.

Consider what children are actually learning in these scenarios, all of which are happening in ordinary families right now:

The parent who tells their child "use your words, not your fists" during sibling conflict while screaming at their spouse during adult conflict is not teaching conflict management. They are teaching that emotional regulation is a rule for children, not a practice for humans: that the real way adults handle conflict is by whoever has the most power wins.

The parent who insists their child deliver a sincere apology after hurting a friend while never, not once, apologizing to their own children for losing their temper or being unfair is not teaching accountability. They are teaching that accountability flows downward: that people with power hold people without power responsible, and that is the entire direction the arrow points.

The parent who coaches their child on managing anxiety while privately catastrophizing every challenge, never sleeping, running on constant stress, and treating every obstacle as a potential catastrophe is not teaching emotional regulation. They are demonstrating that managing anxiety is an aspiration that does not actually survive contact with real life. The child learns both the lesson and the meta-lesson: what adults say and what adults do are different things, and the meta-lesson is what matters.

Children are not listening to what we say nearly as much as they are watching what we do. And they are watching everything.

Teresa was a therapist, she knew all of this intellectually, and she still missed it for years. She had worked hard to teach her son, Daniel, to apologize sincerely when he hurt someone. She coached him through it after every conflict with his younger sister. What she had not noticed was that she had never once apologized to him. Not for losing her temper. Not for the times she had been impatient or unfair. She had explained, justified, redirected: but never said the actual words. One evening Daniel came to her after a blowup and said, in a tone that was genuinely curious rather than accusatory: "Mom, how come I have to apologize but you never do?" She stood in her kitchen and felt the full weight of the question. The next morning she knocked on his door and said, "I've been thinking about what you said. You're right. I'm sorry." He looked at her for a moment, then said, "Thanks, Mom." She said it was the most effective parenting she had ever done. It took about forty seconds.

The Inheritance We Did Not Ask For

Before we go any further with what you should do differently, let us spend a moment with something important: most of what you are modeling right now, for better and for worse, is not original material.

You are, in large part, modeling what was modeled for you.

The emotional patterns you carry, the ways you handle anger, the relationship you have with vulnerability, the degree to which you can sit with uncertainty or discomfort, the instinctive response you have when someone criticizes you, the strategies you reach for when you are overwhelmed, most of these were not chosen. They were absorbed. From your parents, who absorbed them from their parents, who absorbed them from theirs.

Psychologists call this intergenerational transmission of emotional patterns. It is well-documented, deeply researched, and remarkably powerful. Parenting styles, attachment patterns, emotional regulation strategies, conflict behaviors: these pass from generation to generation with striking fidelity, not through genetics alone but through the lived experience of being raised by someone who was raised by someone who was raised by someone.

The parent who grew up in a home where conflict meant explosion learns, at a neurological level, that conflict is dangerous and produces danger. They spend their adult life either avoiding conflict at all costs or escalating rapidly because that is the only conflict model they ever had. They did not choose this. It was installed.

The parent who grew up in a home where vulnerability was met with contempt or dismissal learns that vulnerability is dangerous, that needing things is weakness, that self-sufficiency is the only safe mode. They did not choose this either.

Understanding this is not an excuse for perpetuating patterns that damage your children. It is the context that makes changing those patterns possible. You cannot examine what you do not see. You cannot interrupt what you do not understand.

The first step is simply this: look at what was modeled for you. Not with blame or resentment: that is not what this is about. With clear eyes and genuine curiosity. What did the adults in your childhood model about handling anger? About asking for help? About owning mistakes? About expressing love? About handling disappointment?

What are you carrying forward from that inheritance?

What do you want to put down?

These are not comfortable questions. They are, however, the most important questions in this chapter. Because the patterns end when someone decides they end. The generational chain breaks when someone with awareness and intention does the work to break it.

That someone can be you. It is, in fact, why you are reading this book.

Your EQ Ceiling Becomes Their Floor

Here is a frame that tends to land with unusual force for parents who hear it, because it is both sobering and, if you are paying attention, genuinely hopeful:

Your current level of emotional intelligence is approximately the ceiling of what your child can develop through modeling alone.

They can exceed it. People absolutely grow beyond their upbringing, through their own experiences, through therapy, through the influence of other significant adults, through intentional personal development across a lifetime. The story does not end with childhood. But the default trajectory, without deliberate intervention, is toward what they observed.

If you grew up in a home where feelings were suppressed and you learned to suppress yours, you are modeling emotional suppression for your children. If you grew up where conflict meant whoever was loudest won, you are likely modeling some version of that. If you grew up where vulnerability was dangerous and you learned to be invulnerable, your children are watching you be invulnerable and learning that this is what emotional maturity looks like.

None of this is your fault. You were given a blueprint, and you built from it. You used the tools you had.

But those tools, or the absence of them, are now visible to your children every day. Which means the most important investment you can make in your child's emotional future is not a curriculum or a conversation or a parenting strategy.

It is your own emotional growth.

Consider this an invitation, not a guilt trip. I want to be very clear about that. This is, genuinely, the most hopeful and empowering thing in this entire chapter. Because it means that the work you do on yourself, the therapy, the self-reflection, the hard conversations with your partner about how you both handle stress and conflict and vulnerability, is not separate from parenting. It is parenting. Some of the most consequential parenting you will ever do.

When you do your own work, you are not just becoming better for your own sake. You are raising the ceiling for your children. You are installing updated modeling. You are demonstrating, in the most powerful possible way, that growth is always available, that patterns can be changed, that the way things have always been is not the way they have to be.

You cannot give what you do not have. But you can go get it. And getting it, visibly, imperfectly, persistently, is itself an extraordinary lesson for your children to witness.

ROOT FOUR, CONNECT: What Modeling Looks Like At Each Stage

THE BUILDER (Ages 2–5): The Builder cannot distinguish between what you teach and what you do, for them, those are the same thing. They are not yet capable of noticing hypocrisy or inconsistency in your modeling. What they are absorbing, at a pre-verbal neurological level, is the emotional texture of their home: is this a safe place to have feelings? Do the big people stay calm or do they explode? Do they come back together after conflict or does the air stay cold for days? That texture is installing itself right now. The modeling you do with a Builder is less about specific behaviors and entirely about the emotional climate you create.

THE EXPLORER (Ages 6–10): The Explorer begins to notice the gap between what you say and what you do, and they will tell you about it with the honest, unsparing precision of a child who has not yet learned to be diplomatic. "But you yell when you're mad." This is not defiance. It is observation. Welcome it. "You're right, I do sometimes. That's something I'm working on." The Explorer who sees you acknowledge the gap and commit to working on it learns something more valuable than a perfect model would teach: that growth is ongoing, that noticing is the first step, and that honesty about our shortcomings is not weakness.

THE QUESTIONER (Ages 11–13): The Questioner is conducting a sustained audit of your credibility. They are watching for hypocrisy with forensic precision, and they will find it: because you are human and hypocrisy is inevitable. What matters is not whether you are caught but how you respond when you are. "You're right, I handled that badly" is more powerful than any lecture you will ever deliver. The Questioner who watches a parent own their inconsistencies builds a model of integrity that is far more durable than one built on the illusion of parental perfection.

THE ARCHITECT (Ages 14–17): The Architect is in the process of deciding which parts of you they want to carry forward and which parts they want to reject. This is developmentally appropriate and occasionally brutal. Your modeling now is less about instruction and more about demonstrating who you actually are, your values under pressure, your behavior when no one is grading you, your relationship with your own mistakes. The Architect is taking notes on the person behind the parent. What you model now may not visibly land for years, but it is being archived.

THE LAUNCHER (Ages 18–22): At this stage, the most powerful modeling you can do is living your own life with intention and honesty, showing the Launcher what adult EQ actually looks like in practice. Your conversations become peer-level. They see you navigating work conflict, marriage difficulty, aging parents, personal failure. Every time you handle something with grace, name what you're feeling without drama, or repair something that went wrong, they are seeing a live demonstration of what the skills you tried to teach them look like at full scale. This is the long game paying out.

Think Out Loud

One of the most powerful and most underused modeling strategies available to parents requires nothing more than the willingness to narrate your own emotional experience in real time.

Not performing emotions for educational effect. Not manufacturing feelings for a lesson. Just saying out loud what is actually happening for you as you navigate the ordinary challenges of ordinary days, in a way that makes the invisible visible to the children who are watching.

This sounds simple. For most parents, it is harder than it looks. Many of us were raised in homes where emotional experience was private at best and shameful at worst, where showing feelings was weakness and the appropriate response to difficulty was to handle it quietly and present a composed exterior to the world. Narrating our inner experience out loud, even to our children, feels uncomfortably exposed.

Do it anyway. The discomfort is the work.

Here is what it sounds like in practice:

"I am pretty frustrated right now about a situation at work. Someone gave credit for my project to someone else, and that felt really unfair. I am going to take a walk before I respond to the email so I do not say something I will regret."

What the child just learned: adults get frustrated. Frustration has a name and can be spoken about. There is a gap between feeling something and acting on it. That gap can be used deliberately. Taking a walk is a strategy, not an avoidance. Saying something you will regret is a real risk worth managing.

That is five emotional intelligence lessons in four sentences. No lecture required.

"I said something unkind to your grandmother on the phone this afternoon. I was impatient and I cut her off, and I could hear in her voice that it hurt her. I am going to call her back tonight and apologize."

What the child just learned: adults make mistakes in relationships. Noticing you hurt someone is a skill. Accountability follows noticing, automatically: not defensively, not with a lengthy explanation, just directly. Repair is something you do because it is right, not because you got caught.

None of these narrations are lengthy. None of them require a discussion or a follow-up lesson. They are simply windows into a healthy, functioning emotional life, offered casually, as a matter of course, in the flow of ordinary family life.

The cumulative effect across a childhood of these small narrations is profound. The child builds, gradually and unconsciously, an internal model of what emotional intelligence actually looks like in practice. Not in theory. Not in a book. In a real person, in real time, handling real things.

That model is what they will reach for when they are adults facing their own difficult situations. It is the most practical instruction you will ever give them, and it costs nothing but the willingness to be briefly, appropriately honest.

The Repair Model

Nothing you will ever do as a parent, not the most thoughtful conversation, not the most carefully chosen consequence, not the best book you read to them or the most meaningful trip you take together, is more powerful in its long-term impact on your child's emotional development than this:

Repairing well after you mess up.

Because you will mess up. This is not pessimism. It is arithmetic. You are one person managing the enormous complexity of raising children while also managing a job, a relationship, your own history, your own nervous system, your own unmet needs, and the thousand daily logistics of an actual life. You will lose your temper. You will say the wrong thing. You will be distracted when you needed to be present, harsh when you needed to be gentle, dismissive when you needed to listen, wrong when you were absolutely certain you were right.

This is not a character indictment. It is Tuesday.

The question is not whether you will fail. The question is what you do next.

And what you do next is where the real teaching lives.

When you mess up with your child, when you snap at them unfairly, when you dismiss something that deserved your attention, when you make a judgment call that you later realize was wrong, when you lose your patience in a way that leaves a mark, what you do in the aftermath is teaching them something they will carry for the rest of their lives.

If you walk it back with a real repair, if you come back to them, sit down, and say something like: "I lost my temper earlier and I took it out on you, and that was not fair. You did not deserve that. I am sorry.", you are teaching something extraordinary.

You are teaching that mistakes do not define us. That accountability is possible without catastrophe. That relationships can absorb rupture and come back stronger for having navigated it. That love includes honesty, not just warmth. That the people who love you most will tell you the truth about themselves, including the uncomfortable parts.

You are also, quietly, making it safe for your child to do the same thing. Every genuine apology you model is evidence that owning a mistake is survivable, is actually, somehow, more connecting than hiding it would have been. The child who watches their parent repair learns that repair is what you do when you mess up. Not denial. Not blame-shifting. Not pretending it did not happen. Repair.

The parent who never admits fault in front of their children raises children for whom admission of fault feels like annihilation: because they have never seen evidence that you can do it and survive, let alone that the relationship comes out the other side intact and often stronger.

The parent who repairs consistently raises children who know, at a cellular level, that owning a mistake is not the end of anything. It is the beginning of something better. Because they have watched the person they love most do it, over and over again, without the sky falling.

Repair is the curriculum. Show them how it is done.

CONNECT: Repair Modeling At Each Stage

THE BUILDER (Ages 2–5): Builders cannot process verbal apologies in the adult sense, but they register emotional repair immediately and physically. After a moment where you lost it, raised voice, harsh tone, frustrated reaction, come back quickly. Get down to their level. Soft voice. Steady eyes. "I was too loud. I'm not upset at you. We're okay." Physical warmth if they accept it. The repair is felt before it is understood. That felt sense of safety restored is the entire lesson at this stage.

THE EXPLORER (Ages 6–10): The Explorer can now process a full verbal repair and will remember it. Use all five components: what happened, your responsibility, the impact on them, what you'll do differently, and the explicit restoration of the relationship. "I snapped at you when you were just asking a question, and that wasn't fair. I was stressed and I took it out on you. I'm sorry. That's on me, not you." Watch what happens to their face. The relief when a child sees their parent take full accountability without hedging is visible and immediate.

THE QUESTIONER (Ages 11–13): The Questioner may appear unmoved by your repair, may even seem contemptuous of it. Do it anyway. They are tracking it. Their apparent indifference is a developmental pose, not an accurate signal of impact. The repairs you make during the Questioner years are deposited into an account that pays dividends during the Architect years, when the relationship needs to survive real strain. Every genuine repair says: this relationship can hold hard things. That message accumulates.

THE ARCHITECT (Ages 14–17): Repair with an Architect requires real humility, because the stakes are higher and their capacity for grievance is fully adult. A dismissive or half-hearted repair will make things worse. A genuine one, specific, without excuse, that demonstrates you actually understand the impact, is one of the most connecting things that can happen between a parent and a teenager. "I said that to control you and it wasn't respectful. You deserved better from me." Full stop. No "but." The "but" cancels everything before it.

THE LAUNCHER (Ages 18–22): Repairing with a Launcher means treating them as an adult whose experience of you matters and whose perspective on what happened deserves respect. The most healing repairs at this stage often acknowledge patterns, not just incidents: "I think I've sometimes been more focused on the outcome than on how you were feeling, and I want you to know I see that now." Long-game repair. Worth the vulnerability.

The Mirror Moment

Here is a practice worth building deliberately into your life as a parent. It takes thirty seconds. It is quietly transformative.

Periodically, in the car after a hard moment, at the end of a difficult day, in the private space before you go to sleep, ask yourself honestly:

"If my child grows up to handle this situation exactly the way I just handled it, will I be proud of that?"

Not proud in the public, performative way. Proud in the quiet, private, between-you-and-yourself way that cannot be faked.

Sometimes the answer will be yes. Genuinely yes, I handled that well, I stayed regulated, I was honest without being harsh, I modeled something I would be glad to see in them. Sit with that for a moment. Celebrate it, even privately. It matters.

Sometimes the answer will be no. I lost it. I was dismissive. I said something I did not mean and did not repair it. I modeled exactly the thing I have been trying to teach them not to do.

When the answer is no, the response is not self-punishment. The response is information. What would I have needed in order to handle that differently? More sleep? More support? A pause I did not take? A regulation strategy I have not yet developed? This is diagnostic, not damning.

The mirror question works because it bypasses the self-justification that makes it so easy to rationalize our own worst behavior. You cannot argue with it. You either want your child to handle it the way you handled it, or you do not. The answer is usually obvious.

A Word About Perfection

This chapter is not asking you to be a perfect emotional model. I want to be explicit about that because the preceding pages could reasonably produce that misreading, and nothing in this book will undermine you faster than the belief that you are supposed to be getting this right all the time.

Perfect parents do not exist. And even if they did, they would be genuinely harmful to children. Children need to see adults struggle. They need to see adults fail. They need to see adults face difficulty and uncertainty and loss and not have it all figured out, and keep going anyway.

A child raised by a parent who appeared to always have it together, who never modeled uncertainty or struggle or genuine emotional difficulty, would grow up with a profoundly distorted picture of what adult life looks like, and would be catastrophically unprepared for the reality of it.

The point is not perfection. The point is honesty.

Honest about your own emotional patterns: where you learned them, how they serve you, where they fall short. Honest with your children about when you get it wrong, which you will do regularly and that is okay. Honest about the gap between who you are right now and who you are working to become, and willing to let your children see you working on it.

That honesty, modeled consistently, imperfectly, persistently, is one of the most emotionally intelligent things you can do as a parent.

Your kid is watching. Make it worth watching.

Chapter Three takes the next step: once you are modeling honestly, you need a home environment where honesty is genuinely safe. Because modeling only works if children feel safe enough to follow your lead.

TOOLS FOR CHAPTER TWO

The Think-Aloud Practice Once a day, just once, it does not need to be elaborate, narrate an emotional experience out loud in front of your child. Keep it brief, genuine, and age-appropriate. "I am feeling frustrated about something that happened today and I am going to take a few minutes before I respond." No lesson attached. No follow-up discussion required. Just modeling. Commit to thirty days of this and pay attention to what shifts, in your children, and in yourself.

The Repair Script After any moment where you handled something poorly with your child, come back with a full repair: Name specifically what happened. Take complete responsibility without qualifications. Acknowledge the impact on your child. State what you will do differently. Then follow through, because the follow-through is what gives the repair its meaning. Practice this until it is automatic. The first few times will feel uncomfortable and exposed. That feeling means it is real, and real is what makes it powerful.

The Intergenerational Pattern Audit Set aside thirty minutes with a journal. Ask yourself: what did the adults in my childhood model about handling anger? About asking for help? About admitting they were wrong? About expressing love? About managing disappointment? Write honestly. Then ask: which of those patterns am I still running? Which ones do I want to carry forward? Which ones end with me? This is not about blame. It is about seeing clearly so you can choose deliberately.

The Mirror Question Post this somewhere you will see it regularly, phone lock screen, bathroom mirror, the inside of a cabinet: "Would I be proud if my child handles this exactly the way I just did?" Check in with it weekly. Let the honest answers inform your growth priorities. This question, asked regularly, is one of the most effective personal development tools a parent has access to.

Your Own EQ Inventory Honestly assess yourself on Goleman's five components: self-awareness, self-regulation, motivation, empathy, and social skills. Rate yourself 1 to 5 on each, and be genuinely honest rather than generous. Where are you strongest? Where are the gaps? Identify one specific thing you can do in the next thirty days to develop in your lowest area: a book, a therapy session, a conversation you have been avoiding, a practice you commit to. This is not a one-time exercise. Revisit it every six months. Your EQ is not fixed. Neither is theirs.

CHAPTER THREE

Safety First: Creating a Home Where Truth Wins

The Five Roots this chapter develops: **CONNECT · REPAIR**

Let's do a thought experiment. A quick one. Bear with me.

Imagine you made a significant mistake at work. Not a minor slip: a real one. Something that cost time, money, or credibility. Maybe you sent the wrong report to the wrong client. Maybe you missed a deadline that mattered. Maybe you made a call that turned out to be badly wrong and people noticed.

Now imagine two different bosses you could be walking toward with this information.

Boss A is the kind of person whose emotional state becomes your problem the moment something goes wrong. When they find out about a mistake, they escalate. They lecture. They bring it up again in the next meeting, and the one after that, inserting it into conversations where it is not technically relevant because it is still very much relevant to them. Their disappointment has a half-life measured in weeks. The memory of how they respond to bad news lingers in your body long before you ever walk into their office: a kind of anticipatory dread that has been calibrated by experience.

Boss B finds out about the same mistake. They take a visible breath. They ask what happened, in a tone that is genuinely interested rather than already prosecutorial. They work through it with you: what went wrong, what the impact was, what can be done now, what will be done differently. They are honest that this is not ideal. But when the conversation ends, it ends. The matter is addressed and closed. The professional relationship is intact. You leave their office feeling like an adult who made a mistake, not a criminal who got caught.

Which boss do you tell the truth to?

Which boss do you come to early, before the mistake has compounded, before the cover-up has created a second problem on top of the first? Which boss gets accurate information about what is actually happening in real time, and which one gets a carefully managed version designed to minimize your exposure?

The answer is obvious. And it is exactly the calculation your child is making about you, every single day.

Every child is continuously and unconsciously assessing the emotional environment of their home and arriving at a conclusion about what happens when they are honest. Whether the truth is safe here. Whether the cost of admission is worth the price. Whether the person they need to tell is Boss A or Boss B.

And they are making their decisions about truth-telling, blame, concealment, and accountability based entirely on that assessment: not on the values you have stated, not on the rules you have posted, not on the lectures you have delivered about honesty being important.

On the environment they have actually experienced.

The environment creates the behavior. Every time. Without exception.

A mother named Priya found this out the hard way. Her twelve-year-old son, Aiden, had been hiding a failing grade in math for two months: a full quarter. By the time it surfaced, the hole was deep enough that summer school was on the table. Priya was furious. And then, in a quiet moment, she asked him honestly: "Why didn't you tell me?" He looked at her and said, "Because last year when I failed the spelling test you yelled for like an hour." She had no memory of the incident. He remembered every word.

She realized she had trained him, without meaning to, to hide bad news. The consequence she thought she had delivered for a failed spelling test had actually been delivered for honesty. She had accidentally taught him that the safe move was silence. Rebuilding took months. It started with one sentence: "I need you to know that I want you to come to me when things go wrong, not after. I'm not going to be perfect about my reaction, but I'm going to keep trying. Deal?" He looked skeptical. She didn't blame him. But he said deal.

Why Kids Really Lie

When a child lies or deflects blame, the easiest and least useful interpretation is the character interpretation: they are sneaky, manipulative, untrustworthy, lacking integrity. This interpretation is satisfying in a certain way because it locates the problem entirely in the child and leaves the environment, and the parent's contribution to it, entirely unexamined.

It is also, for the vast majority of lying and blame-deflecting behavior, simply wrong.

Understanding what is actually driving the behavior is not about excusing it. The behavior still needs to be addressed, consequences still apply, and accountability still matters. But the intervention that actually works has to target the real cause. Treating anxiety as defiance, treating shame as dishonesty, treating rational self-protection as a character failure: these approaches whack the symptom while the root cause continues to grow.

Here is what is actually going on most of the time:

Fear of consequence. The most common driver of children's lying, by a substantial margin, is simple fear. The truth feels catastrophic, disproportionately catastrophic given the actual severity of the mistake, and the lie feels like the only viable escape route. This is almost never a character problem. It is almost always an environment problem. The question worth asking is not "why did they lie?" but "what did they believe would happen if they told the truth?"

Shame rather than guilt. This distinction is so important to this chapter, and to this entire book, that we will spend significant time on it. For now: when a child has come to associate their mistakes with their fundamental worth as a person rather than with specific behaviors, the drive to hide those mistakes becomes nearly overwhelming. They are not protecting a lie. They are protecting their sense of self. That is a survival instinct, not a character deficiency.

Watching adults model it. Children who grow up watching the adults in their lives routinely deflect responsibility, construct elaborate justifications for their own bad behavior, tell convenient versions of the truth, and treat accountability as something that applies to other people learn, with straightforward observational efficiency, that this is how humans manage mistakes. We examined this in Chapter Two. It bears repeating here because it is directly relevant: if you want your child to tell the truth, you need to model telling the truth. Including about your own mistakes. Including when it costs you something.

Protecting the relationship. This one surprises parents. Particularly with older children and teenagers, some lying is motivated not by self-interest but by a genuine desire to protect the parent: not to disappoint them, not to burden them, not to add to stress that already seems significant. The impulse underneath this lying is actually loving. It is also, of course, a sign that the child does not yet trust that the relationship can handle the truth. That is its own important information.

Developmental immaturity. Young children, particularly under seven, are not always lying in the way adults mean when they use that word. They live in the immediate moment. The lie works right now and avoids an unpleasant outcome right now, and the downstream consequences, damaged trust, compounding complexity, the inevitable discovery, are simply not yet real to them in the way they become real later. This is not moral failure. It is where they are developmentally. The response is teaching, not punishing.

The cause shapes the solution. Treating every lie as strategic deception rather than self-protection, fear management, or developmental limitation means you will be having the same conversation, with escalating frustration, for years, while the underlying driver remains unaddressed and undisturbed.

Building a Truth-Safe Environment

The single most powerful thing you can do to reduce lying, blame-deflecting, and concealment in your home does not involve consequences, detection strategies, or emotional appeals to your child's better nature.

It involves changing what it costs to tell the truth.

Specifically: making honesty consistently, demonstrably, and reliably safer than deception. Not in theory. In practice. In the actual lived experience of what happens in your home when someone comes to you with something difficult.

This starts with a policy, stated explicitly, not just implied:

"In this family, I will always be more upset about a lie than about the original mistake. If you come to me with the truth, we deal with it together. If I find out you lied, the lie becomes its own problem on top of whatever happened. I would rather know the hard truth than find out later you hid it from me."

Say this. More than once. In different ways, across different years, at different developmental stages. Make it a family norm so thoroughly embedded that it does not need to be restated: it is simply understood as the operating culture of your household.

And then, this is the part that is harder than saying it, you have to prove it. Every single time.

Because here is the truth about truth-safe environments: they are built or destroyed one interaction at a time. Every time your child comes to you with something difficult and your response is regulated, curious, and proportional, you add one brick to the truth-safe structure. Every time your child comes to you with something difficult and your response is an explosion, a lecture that lasts forty-five minutes, or a punishment that feels wildly disproportionate to a confession that required real courage, you knock several bricks out.

Children are keeping score. Not consciously, not maliciously, just adaptively, the way any organism calibrates its behavior to the actual conditions of its environment rather than the stated conditions. If the actual conditions say that honesty produces danger, they will treat honesty as dangerous regardless of what the stated conditions say.

This does not mean there are no consequences when things go wrong. Consequences are appropriate, important, and part of how children learn that actions have impact. What it means is that the consequence for truth is consistently, meaningfully lighter than the consequence for deception. The child who comes to you and says "I broke the vase and I was scared to tell you but I knew I had to" should experience a fundamentally different consequence than the child who broke the vase, denied it, blamed the dog, and got caught in the lie. Not because the vase matters differently, but because the honesty matters more.

Every parent who consistently honors that principle is building a child who comes to them before things get catastrophic: because coming forward feels safer than hiding. That child is not just more honest. They are safer. They are the teenager who tells you about the party that got out of hand instead of managing it alone. They are the young adult who calls you when they are in over their head instead of waiting until the situation has become a crisis. The truth-safe environment you build now has returns that pay out for decades.

CONNECT: Building a Truth-Safe Environment At Each Stage

THE BUILDER (Ages 2–5): Builders lie instinctively and without guile, "I didn't eat the cookie" with chocolate on their face is not deception, it is developmental. They are testing cause and effect, not plotting against you. Your response to these early untruths sets the tone for everything that follows. Keep consequences mild and consistent. Never make them feel caught in a trap. "I can see what happened. Let's talk about it", warm, matter-of-fact, not catastrophic, is the foundation of the truth-safe home. They are learning: when I tell the truth here, the world stays intact.

THE EXPLORER (Ages 6–10): This is the stage to explicitly establish the truth policy as a family value. Name it, explain it, and most importantly, demonstrate it. "In our family, the truth always costs less than the lie." Explorers can understand this as a rule, a contract, a family standard, and they respond well to the clear structure of it. When they do come forward with something honest that cost them something to admit, make a visible, genuine deal of it: "I know that was hard to tell me. Thank you for trusting me with it." That recognition is the deposit that builds the account.

THE QUESTIONER (Ages 11–13): Truth-safety is stress-tested hard at this stage. The Questioner is navigating peer culture, identity formation, and the beginning of a private inner life that they are appropriately not sharing entirely with you. Some concealment at this stage is healthy developmental boundary-setting, not dishonesty. The key is keeping the door open for the things that matter: "You don't have to tell me everything. But if you're in trouble or you're scared, I want to be the person you come to. I will deal with it, I won't fall apart." Repeat this across the years. It is a promissory note they will cash when they need it most.

THE ARCHITECT (Ages 14–17): The stakes of truth-safety peak here. The things Architects conceal, substance use, relationship difficulty, mental health struggles, situations that have gotten genuinely out of hand, have real consequences. Your response to the first major disclosure will determine whether future disclosures happen. If the first big truth they tell you is met with an explosion, a withdrawal of trust, or consequences disproportionate to the honesty it took to come forward, you have just communicated: do not do that again. Regulate yourself, ask questions before reacting, and remember that knowing is always better than not knowing.

THE LAUNCHER (Ages 18–22): The Launcher's truth-safety is now about the quality of the adult relationship you are building. Are you someone they can call when things go wrong, really wrong, without fearing your reaction? That relationship is built on everything that came before, but it is also still being built right now. The parent who responds to a Launcher's difficult disclosure with curiosity and steadiness rather than panic and control is the parent who gets the next call, and the one after that.

The Shame-Guilt Distinction: The Most Important Page in This Chapter

Brené Brown has spent decades researching shame, vulnerability, and what she calls "wholehearted living," and her findings on shame are among the most practically significant in the popular psychology literature.

Shame does not improve behavior. This is the finding. Brené Brown's research at the University of Houston, spanning over a decade of interviews and qualitative studies on shame and vulnerability, reaches this conclusion explicitly and with force: shame, as a motivational force, does not make people better. It makes them worse. Specifically, it makes them more likely to hide, more likely to repeat the shamed behavior in secret, more likely to develop rigid defensive patterns that protect against future shame exposure, and more likely to turn the shame outward as aggression, blame, or contempt.

This is not how we use shame culturally. We use it as a behavior modification tool, constantly and reflexively. We shame children into compliance, adults into correction, communities into adherence to norms. We do this because it appears to work in the immediate moment: the shamed person stops the behavior, or at least performs stopping it. What we do not see, because it happens internally and over time, is the cost.

The critical distinction, and it is one that parents have enormous influence over, is between shame and guilt.

Guilt says: I did something bad. It is behavior-focused. It is uncomfortable, yes, genuinely uncomfortable, as it should be, but it is survivable. It points outward, toward the action and its impact. And because it is oriented toward a behavior rather than a self, it motivates repair. I did something bad, therefore I want to make it right. Guilt is the feeling that drives accountability. It is healthy. It means the moral compass is working. We want our children to feel guilt when they have genuinely wronged someone.

Shame says: I am bad. It is self-focused. It feels like annihilation, like the floor falling out from under your sense of who you are. And because it is oriented toward the self rather than a behavior, it does not motivate repair. There is no repairing a self. There is only protecting it, hiding it, defending it, or, in the cases where it becomes truly overwhelming, attacking others to redirect the unbearable internal experience outward.

The language we use in our corrective moments with children is the lever that determines which of these we activate. And the differences in language are often so subtle that parents deploy shame-activating language without any awareness that they are doing so.

Compare these pairs:

"You are so irresponsible" versus "That was an irresponsible choice." The first attacks the identity. The second addresses the behavior. One activates shame. The other activates guilt. The words are almost identical. The impact is entirely different.

"How could you do something like that?" versus "That behavior caused real harm. Let's talk about what happened." The first implies that the person who did this is fundamentally defective: because a non-defective person could not have done this. The second keeps the focus on the behavior and its consequences, and opens toward repair.

"You always do this" versus "This is the third time this week. What is going on?" The first is almost certainly inaccurate and weaponizes frequency to make a statement about character. The second is specific, factual, and, here is the important word, curious. Curiosity is incompatible with shame. You cannot shame someone and be genuinely curious about them simultaneously.

"I am so disappointed in you" versus "I am disappointed in what happened here. Let's figure out what went wrong." The first makes you the standard against which they are being measured and found wanting. The second makes the situation the problem: which it is.

Every one of these shifts is small. None of them require elaborate rewording or constant vigilance once you understand the principle. The principle is this: keep your corrections aimed at behavior, not identity. Address what happened, not who they are. Reserve your most direct statements for the action and its impact, and your most curious questions for the person.

That distinction, maintained consistently, raises children in guilt rather than shame. And children raised in guilt rather than shame have access to the emotional machinery of accountability. They can own their mistakes because owning a mistake does not mean owning a damaged self. It means acknowledging a specific behavior, repairing its impact, and updating their approach.

That is the whole engine of growth. Shame breaks the engine. Guilt runs it.

Stop the Interrogation

Here is a specific, practical, immediately actionable thing to stop doing:

Stop asking your child if they did something wrong when you already know they did.

"Did you eat the cookies I was saving?": when you watched them through the kitchen doorway eat the cookies.

"Did you hit your sister?": when your sister is standing in front of you with a red mark on her arm and tears on her face.

"Did you finish your homework?": when you have already checked the app that shows you exactly what was submitted and when.

This is a trap. Not a malicious trap, usually: it is deployed reflexively, out of habit, because it is how we were spoken to and because somewhere we have absorbed the idea that a confession is more valuable than a fact. But the trap is real: you are presenting the child with a binary that they did not create and that rewards lying.

They can tell the truth and face whatever consequence awaits. Or they can lie and at least delay the consequence, buy some time, and maybe, in the best case scenario from where they are standing, avoid it altogether if their version holds. For a child who has not yet built complete confidence that truth is safe, the lie is a rational gamble. You just set it up for them.

Remove the question. Replace it with the acknowledgment.

"I know you ate the cookies. I'm not as upset about the cookies as I am about why you thought that was okay when we had talked about it. Tell me what was going on."

"I saw what happened between you two. Come sit down and let's talk about it."

"I checked, and the homework isn't submitted. Let's figure out what happened."

What you have done here is several things simultaneously. You have removed the incentive to lie by removing the possibility of the lie working. You have signaled that you are interested in understanding rather than simply prosecuting. You have kept the conversation focused on behavior and thinking rather than creating a moment where the child's survival instincts are fully engaged before the conversation even begins.

A child in survival mode cannot learn. A child who does not need to survive the conversation can.

Blaming: The Other Side of the Same Coin

Lying hides a mistake. Blaming relocates it. Both serve the same protective function, keeping the self insulated from accountability, and both are driven by the same underlying fear that accountability is annihilating.

"It was his fault." "She made me do it." "I would have done better if you had not interrupted me." "The teacher has it out for me." "Everyone else was doing it."

These are not, primarily, lies. They may contain some elements of truth. But they are deflections, strategic or instinctive relocations of responsibility away from the self and onto the environment, other people, circumstances, anything that is not I made this choice and it had this impact.

Left unchallenged, this pattern solidifies into something much more serious than a child's defensive habit. It becomes a worldview: I am not the author of my own outcomes. Things happen to me. Other people determine what happens in my life. When things go well it is because I was capable; when things go badly it is because the circumstances, other people, or the universe conspired against me.

Adults who operate from this worldview, and there are many, many of them, and you have almost certainly worked with some and perhaps been in relationship with some, are characterized by a particular combination of chronic frustration and genuine bewilderment. They cannot understand why their relationships keep not working. They cannot see their own role in the patterns that repeat in their lives. They cannot grow in the ways that matter because growth requires acknowledging that you have something to do with your outcomes, and that acknowledgment is precisely what the worldview forecloses.

The time to interrupt this pattern is in childhood. Not with punishment or shame, we just covered why that backfires. But with a consistent, calm, genuinely curious redirection to the one question that matters above all others in these moments:

"What was your part in this?"

Not "was this your fault?" Not an accusation dressed as a question. A genuine inquiry into what role, however small, however real, however mixed with the genuine contributions of others and genuine unfairness of circumstance, the child played in what happened.

Because there is almost always a part. Even in situations where the other person's behavior was genuinely worse. Even where the circumstances were genuinely unfair. Even where the child was, in important ways, a victim of something real. There is still almost always a part: a choice made, a moment responded to, an action taken or not taken that contributed to the outcome.

Helping children find and own that part, without minimizing what others did, without denying genuine unfairness, without blaming them for the entirety of a complex situation, is teaching them agency. The understanding that they are not only acted upon but also acting. Not only recipients of their circumstances but also contributors to them.

That understanding is the foundation of every meaningful change a person ever makes in their own life. It is the opposite of victimhood. And it can only be built by someone who is willing to ask, patiently and repeatedly and without judgment, what was your part?

The Curiosity Stance

The single most useful orientation a parent can bring to a moment of dishonesty, blame, or concealment is genuine curiosity.

Not performed curiosity. Not the diagnostic curiosity of a detective building a case. Not even the therapeutic curiosity of someone who has read enough books to know that asking open-ended questions is good practice. Actual, warm, interested curiosity about what was happening inside your child that led to this moment.

Because here is what curiosity does that nothing else can: it communicates that the person asking is genuinely more interested in understanding than in judging. And a child who feels genuinely seen and genuinely understood, even in their most difficult, least flattering moments, does not need to hide. The hiding is a defense against a threat, and when the curiosity is real, the threat does not materialize.

“Help me understand what was going on for you.”

"What were you thinking when you made that choice?"

"What did you think was going to happen?"

"What were you scared of?"

These questions do not excuse behavior. They do not reduce consequences or communicate that what happened was acceptable. They create the conditions in which the behavior can be honestly examined by the child rather than defended against or denied. And a behavior that can be honestly examined can be understood, and a behavior that can be understood can be changed.

The child who feels genuinely understood, even when they are in trouble, even when they did something wrong, even when the conversation is hard, is the child who comes to you next time before the thing has gotten out of hand. Because coming to you feels like coming to someone who wants to understand, not someone who wants to punish.

That is what safety makes possible. Not a home where there are no consequences. A home where the truth is always the best available option, because the person you are bringing it to is curious rather than catastrophizing, interested rather than inflamed, and genuinely more concerned with understanding you than with managing their own feelings about what you did.

That home produces honest children. Honest children become honest adults.

It is the whole game.

CONNECT + REPAIR: Curiosity Over Interrogation At Each Stage

THE BUILDER (Ages 2–5): With Builders, curiosity looks like staying warm and physical during a truth moment rather than stiffening into authority. Get down to their level. Keep your voice soft and genuinely interested. "What happened here? Tell me." Not as a trap, as a real question. The content of their answer matters less than the experience of being asked with warmth. You are teaching them that coming to you feels safe.

THE EXPLORER (Ages 6–10): Explorers can handle, and benefit from, the full curiosity practice. "Help me understand what you were thinking" is a question they will actually engage with if you ask it genuinely. At this age, they are often genuinely puzzled by their own choices and will walk you through their in-the-moment reasoning with surprising candor if you are not visibly angry. The curiosity opens the hood. What you find under the hood is almost always more useful than what the behavior looked like from the outside.

THE QUESTIONER (Ages 11–13): Curiosity is the only tool that consistently gets through at this stage. Accusation, interrogation, and visible disappointment all trigger shutdown or defense. "I'm not here to catch you out, I just want to understand", and meaning it, is the posture that keeps the conversation alive. You will not always get full honesty from a Questioner. But genuine curiosity will get you more than anything else will, and it keeps the relationship intact for the next conversation.

THE ARCHITECT (Ages 14–17): The Architect's interior life is complex, actively private, and often genuinely ambivalent, they are not always sure themselves why they did what they did. Curiosity that is patient enough to sit with "I don't know" without treating it as deflection is the advanced practice here. "That's okay. Think about it and let me know when you have a theory", and then actually returning to it later, is more productive than forcing an answer in the hot moment. The conversation that happens two days later, when defenses are down, is often the real one.

THE LAUNCHER (Ages 18–22): Curiosity with a Launcher means resisting the impulse to advise, fix, or editorialize when they come to you with something difficult. "Tell me more about that" and "What was that like for you?", asked without an agenda, will get you further into genuine understanding than any question that contains the shape of the answer you were expecting. The Launcher who feels genuinely understood, not managed, is the one who keeps coming back.

Safety and truth are the container. Chapter Four looks at what goes inside it: the single most important skill in the entire emotional intelligence stack: the ability to pause before you react. Without regulation, everything else in this book is theory.

TOOLS FOR CHAPTER THREE

The Truth Contract Have an explicit, age-appropriate family conversation about your truth policy, not as a lecture but as a genuine agreement. State it clearly: in this family, I will always be more upset about a lie than about the original mistake. Honesty always costs less than deception. Revisit this contract when there is a breach, not as a "gotcha" but as a reminder of the agreement you both made. Let the policy be alive, referenced, and real, not just words said once and forgotten.

The Non-Interrogation Habit For one week, practice catching yourself before you ask a question you already know the answer to, and replace the question with an acknowledgment. "I know what happened. I want to understand why." Track how often you were about to set up the trap. The awareness itself changes the behavior. The new pattern, acknowledgment followed by curiosity, produces conversations instead of interrogations.

The Blame Redirect When your child deflects to blame, which they will, regularly, because this is what children do, establish one consistent, neutral, genuinely curious phrase: "I hear that. What was your part?" Practice the tone until it is genuinely curious rather than sarcastically loaded. The question itself, asked with real interest over many years, teaches agency more effectively than any lecture about personal responsibility ever could.

Shame vs. Guilt Language Audit For one week, pay close attention to your corrective language. After each correction, ask yourself: did that statement target a behavior, or did it target a person? Did it activate guilt, I did something wrong, or shame, I am something wrong? Start building the habit of behavior-specific corrections: "That choice was unkind" rather than "You are so unkind." The shift is small and the impact is enormous, accumulated across years.

The Curiosity Practice The next time your child lies, deflects, or blames, try leading entirely with curiosity before any consequence or correction. "Help me understand what was going on for you." Listen to the full answer before responding. Notice what the curiosity reveals that accusation would have buried. This does not mean no consequences follow, they may. But the conversation that happens before the consequence determines whether the child learns something or simply survives the interaction and files you under "Boss A."

PART TWO: THE CORE SKILLS

CHAPTER FOUR

The Pause: Teaching Self-Regulation Before It's Needed

The Five Roots this chapter develops: **REGULATE · NOTICE**

It is 6:47 on a Wednesday evening.

Your ten-year-old has just lost a video game he has been working toward for forty-five minutes. He throws the controller. It hits the wall. There is a new mark on the paint. He is now screaming, not words exactly, more of a pressurized sound, and his face is a color that suggests his cardiovascular system is deeply involved.

You have had, by rough estimate, eleven hours of your own day by this point. You are tired in the specific way that parents of school-age children are tired, which is the kind of tired that has layers. You have not eaten dinner. You had your own difficult thing happen at work that you have not had space to process. And now there is a hole in the wall, or at least a mark, and a child making that sound.

What you do in the next sixty seconds will teach him something. The question is what.

If you match his energy, if the adrenaline already running in your system catches his adrenaline and they compound each other and suddenly you are both escalating in a room that has too much activation in it, you will teach him that overwhelming emotion is contagious, that adults also lose control, and that the appropriate response to a dysregulated child is more dysregulation.

If you go cold, if you shut down, go flat, impose a consequence with zero relational warmth, you will teach him that feelings are not welcome here and that the way to manage someone else's emotional overwhelm is to withdraw from it entirely.

If you can find the pause, if you can locate, in a body that is also activated, the regulated presence that the moment actually requires, you will teach him something worth far more than whatever consequence follows. You will teach him that overwhelming emotion is survivable, that it has a shape and a duration, that the people who love you do not abandon you in it, and that there is something on the other side of the storm besides wreckage.

The pause is not a parenting technique. It is a capacity. And like all capacities, it is built, in yourself first, and then, through everything covered in this chapter, in your child.

What Self-Regulation Actually Is (And Is Not)

Before we build the capacity, we need to be precise about what we are actually building, because self-regulation is one of the most misunderstood concepts in the entire emotional intelligence space.

Self-regulation is not emotional suppression. This distinction is not a nuance: it is the whole thing, and confusing the two produces outcomes that are directly opposite of what parents want.

Suppression is the internal instruction: do not feel that. Push it down. Override it. Present a composed exterior regardless of what is happening inside. Suppression is the emotional equivalent of putting a lid on a pot that is boiling and turning up the heat. The contents do not stop boiling. The pressure builds. Eventually, the lid comes off, usually at the worst possible moment, usually with more force than the original situation warranted, usually directed at whoever happens to be standing nearest when the system reaches its limit.

James Gross at Stanford has spent decades studying exactly this, and his research is unambiguous: habitual emotional suppression is associated with significantly higher physiological stress responses, worse memory consolidation, lower reported wellbeing, worse relationship quality, and greater likelihood of emotional dysregulation events. The people who are working hardest to appear calm are often, physiologically, the least calm. The system does not forget what it was told to ignore. It just holds it somewhere else.

Self-regulation is categorically different. Self-regulation does not say do not feel that. It says: I feel that. I know what it is. Now I am going to do something deliberate with the space between feeling it and acting on it.

The pressure is still there. The steam is real. But there is a functioning valve, and someone with a hand on it making a conscious choice about when and how to release it rather than waiting for the system to blow.

The goal of self-regulation, what we are building in our children when we do this work well, is not children who do not feel things intensely. It is children who feel things intensely and have increasing command over what they do with those feelings. Children who can be moved without being swept away. Children who can be angry and not destructive, anxious and not avoidant, sad and not collapsed, excited and not reckless.

That is the capacity. That is what the pause makes possible.

A father named James described what this looked like in practice, not when he got it right, but the day he finally understood what he had been getting wrong. His thirteen-year-old, Elijah, had come home from school wound tight, slammed his bag down, and refused to talk. James's instinct was to demand an explanation. He had spent the day working. He was also tired. He started to escalate, and then caught something in himself. He felt the pull toward the lecture, toward "you don't get to come in here and," and he stopped. He went to the kitchen, poured two glasses of water, put one in front of Elijah, and sat down without saying anything. He stayed there. After about four minutes, he clocked it, Elijah said, "This kid keeps humiliating me in front of everyone and nobody does anything." James didn't solve it. He said, "That sounds exhausting." And Elijah talked for twenty minutes. James told me: "I realized that what he needed wasn't a response. He needed to find out that I could handle it: that I wasn't going to make it worse. Once he knew that, he could actually talk." The pause wasn't silence. It was a signal: I'm regulated. You can be too.

Inside the Flooded Brain

Understanding what is actually happening neurologically when a child, or an adult, is in the grip of an overwhelming emotional state changes how you respond to it. It shifts the frame from this child is choosing to behave badly to this child's brain is in a state where better behavior is currently neurologically unavailable.

That shift matters enormously. Not as an excuse: the behavior still has consequences, and the child still needs to develop regulatory capacity. But as context for what kind of intervention is actually possible in the moment.

Here is what is happening:

When the amygdala detects something it registers as a threat, and the threat can be physical, social, emotional, symbolic, or anything the nervous system has been trained to treat as dangerous, it initiates a cascade. Stress hormones flood the system. The body prepares for fight, flight, or freeze. Blood flow is redirected from the prefrontal cortex, the reasoning, perspective-taking, language-processing, impulse-controlling center, toward the motor systems and the survival-relevant processing centers.

The thinking brain, in a very real neurological sense, goes offline. Not completely, not permanently, but substantially. The capacity for rational thought, for imagining consequences, for perspective-taking, for using language to process experience, all of it reduces dramatically.

Daniel Goleman called this the amygdala hijack. The survival brain takes the wheel. And the survival brain, for all its extraordinary efficiency at keeping us alive under genuine threat, is not particularly interested in nuance, proportionality, long-term thinking, or the relational consequences of what it is about to do. It wants the threat to stop. Right now. By whatever means are most immediately available.

For a ten-year-old who lost a video game, the "threat" the amygdala registered was probably something like: I failed, I am incompetent, my effort was wasted, this is intolerable. The emotional experience, the humiliation, the frustration, the sense of unfairness, is completely real. The amygdala's response to it is completely proportional given what it perceives. The controller hits the wall because the survival brain has the wheel and it wants the intolerable feeling to stop.

You cannot reason with that brain. You cannot lecture it, consequence it effectively, or redirect it while it is fully in that state. None of this is a statement about the child's character or your parenting. It is a statement about neurology.

What you can do, what is actually possible in that moment, is help the nervous system return to the window of tolerance where the thinking brain can come back online. And then, once it has, the teaching can happen.

The Window of Tolerance

Psychiatrist Dan Siegel's concept of the window of tolerance is one of the most practically useful frameworks in all of developmental psychology, and it is worth understanding clearly because it will change how you read your child's behavior.

The window of tolerance is the zone of optimal arousal: the range of emotional activation within which the brain can function effectively. Inside the window, you can think clearly, access empathy, solve problems, engage with other people, regulate your responses, and learn from your experience. This is the operational range for everything that makes humans capable of sophisticated thought and behavior.

Outside the window, in either direction, that capacity diminishes sharply.

Outside the window upward, into what Siegel calls hyperarousal, is panic, rage, flooding, overwhelm, the explosive response. Everything is too much, too loud, too fast, too threatening. The system is overactivated and cannot access its higher functions.

Outside the window downward, into hypoarousal, is shutdown, numbness, dissociation, the collapse response. The system has been overwhelmed in the other direction and has simply turned off the lights to protect itself. The child who goes completely blank and unresponsive in a difficult moment is not being deliberately difficult. They are outside their window in the other direction.

Children have narrower windows than adults. This is not a defect: it is developmental reality, a direct consequence of having a prefrontal cortex that is still under active construction. The regulatory infrastructure simply has not fully formed yet.

This means that stimuli which would barely nudge an adult's nervous system can genuinely knock a child outside their window. The wrong cup. The difficult homework problem. The moment a sibling gets something they did not get. These seem trivial from the outside. From inside a nervous system with a narrow window and limited regulatory capacity, they are genuinely overwhelming.

Our job, as the adults in the room, is twofold: to help children return to their window when they have been knocked out of it, and to gradually expand their window over time so that it takes more to knock them out and they return more quickly when it does.

Both of these take time. Both require patience and repetition. Neither can be rushed. The window expands through accumulated experience of being regulated with support across years of development: not through punishment for failing to regulate, not through demands for better behavior that the nervous system is not yet equipped to produce.

Co-Regulation: The Most Important Thing In This Chapter

The biological truth that changes everything about how you approach a dysregulated child:

A dysregulated adult cannot regulate a dysregulated child.

Read that again. It is the whole game.

The nervous system does not regulate in isolation. Particularly in early childhood, and to a significant degree throughout childhood and adolescence, the child's nervous system regulates in relationship with the caregiver's nervous system. This is not metaphor. It is measurable, documented, neurobiological reality.

When a regulated adult is present with a dysregulated child, genuinely regulated, not performing calm while internally escalating, the child's nervous system begins to sync with the adult's. Heart rate variability, cortisol levels, breathing patterns, they begin to entrain toward the calmer system. The child literally borrows regulatory capacity from the adult until they have developed enough of their own.

This process, which researchers call co-regulation, is the foundation of every other regulatory skill a child develops. Allan Schore's extensive neuroscience research on right-brain-to-right-brain communication between caregivers and infants shows that the child's developing regulatory systems are literally shaped by repeated experiences of co-regulation with an attuned adult. It is why the quality of early attachment relationships predicts emotional regulation outcomes years and decades later. The child who has consistent access to a regulated, responsive caregiver is building their own regulatory capacity on that foundation. The child who does not have consistent access to that, whose primary caregivers are themselves chronically dysregulated, unavailable, or frightening, is trying to build regulatory capacity without a scaffold.

This has direct, immediate implications for how you walk into a difficult moment with your child.

If your child is dysregulated and you are also dysregulated, which is entirely understandable given that children's dysregulation is specifically designed to activate the nervous systems of the adults around them, because that activation is evolutionarily useful, the first job is yours. Regulate yourself first. Not as a performance. Not by white-knuckling composure while your heart rate climbs. Actually regulate.

Breathe. Genuinely, slowly, deliberately breathe. The physiological sigh, a double inhale through the nose followed by a long, complete exhale through the mouth, activates the parasympathetic nervous system more rapidly than almost any other single technique. Do it before you speak. Do it where your child can see you if possible. Model the regulation in real time.

Take a moment if you need one. "I need a minute before we talk about this" is not avoidance. It is the most regulated, intelligent response available. It is also modeling exactly what you want your child to learn to do: that feelings are manageable, that the pause is possible, that you do not have to respond to the moment with the full force of your activation.

You cannot give your child regulation you do not currently have. But you can get it, quickly, right here, right now. Breathe first. Then engage.

Building the Toolkit: What Actually Works

Self-regulation strategies are not one-size-fits-all. Different children, different temperaments, different nervous system profiles, different developmental stages all call for different approaches. What sends one child back to their window sends another child further outside it.

The goal is not to hand every child the same toolkit. The goal is to help each child build their own: a personal collection of strategies they have actually tried, actually experienced working, and can actually access when they are inside a difficult moment. Not what sounded good in a calm conversation. What works for this specific child in this specific body.

Here is the full range to draw from, organized by type:

Movement-based strategies work by metabolizing the stress hormones, the cortisol, the adrenaline, that are flooding the body during hyperarousal. The body prepared for action; giving it action is efficient and effective. Running, jumping, doing jumping jacks, push-ups against a wall, dancing to a song, hitting a pillow, any vigorous physical movement releases what has built up. This is particularly effective for children who tend toward the explosive, hyperaroused end of dysregulation. If your child's emotional overwhelm tends to look like big physical energy going outward, movement is probably their primary regulatory tool.

Breathing strategies work by directly activating the parasympathetic nervous system, the body's rest-and-digest counterbalance to the fight-or-flight response. The breath is the only autonomic function we can also control voluntarily, which makes it a uniquely accessible regulatory tool. Box breathing, four counts in, four counts hold, four counts out, four counts hold, is the most commonly taught and works well for many children once they have practiced it enough that it is automatic. The physiological sigh is faster and requires less practice: a double inhale through the nose, filling the lungs as completely as possible, followed by a long, slow, complete exhale through the mouth. One or two of these can measurably shift physiological state within seconds.

Sensory strategies work through the sensory input that interrupts the escalation loop, a different signal entering the nervous system that the brain has to process, creating a brief gap in the escalation. Cold water on the face or wrists is particularly effective because the diving reflex, an ancient physiological response to cold water on the face, triggers a rapid decrease in heart rate. A weighted blanket provides deep pressure input that many nervous systems find organizing. Strong flavors, specific textures, particular smells, sensory strategies are highly individual and worth exploring systematically with your child to find what actually works for them.

Cognitive strategies work for older children whose prefrontal cortex is developed enough to use thinking to recruit more prefrontal cortex. Naming what is happening, "this is my amygdala, it is trying to protect me, I am actually safe", requires the language centers and activates the reasoning center simultaneously. Counting backward from one hundred by sevens works because it is difficult enough to require genuine cognitive engagement, which brings the thinking brain back online. The five-four-three-two-one grounding technique, five things you can see, four you can hear, three you can touch, two you can smell, one you can taste, anchors the nervous system in present sensory reality rather than the feared or imagined future that anxiety is usually about.

Connection strategies reflect the fact that for many children, particularly those with secure attachment histories, the fastest route back to their window is through another regulated human being. Some children regulate best through physical proximity and touch: a hug, sitting in a lap, a hand on a shoulder. Others need the presence of a trusted person without necessarily being touched. Know your child. Some children need space first and connection later; some need connection to access space. The question to ask, during a calm moment: when you are really upset, does it help more when I come close or when I give you room? Their answer is the answer.

Creative strategies work because channeling emotional energy into creative expression both releases it and, often, illuminates it. Drawing an angry picture. Writing out the feelings. Building something with hands. Playing an instrument. The creative act gives the energy somewhere to go that produces something rather than destroying something, and the product of the creative act often reveals emotional content that the child could not access directly.

The Critical Rule: Build the Toolkit Before the Crisis

This cannot be overstated. The most common and most counterproductive mistake parents make with regulation strategies is trying to introduce or teach them during a crisis.

It does not work. A child who is outside their window of tolerance, who is flooded, dysregulated, in full amygdala-hijack mode, is not capable of learning a new skill. The learning centers of the brain are among the first things to go offline when the survival brain takes over. You can hand them a breathing card and talk them through box breathing in the middle of a meltdown and accomplish almost nothing, and then wonder why the strategy does not work.

The strategy has to be built during the calm. Practiced during the calm. Made familiar and automatic during the calm. So that when the storm hits, the hand already knows where to reach.

Have the toolkit conversation on a Sunday morning when everyone has had breakfast and nobody is in crisis. "Hey, I have been thinking about what helps you when you are really upset. Can we figure out some things together?" Build the list collaboratively, their input matters, both because they know their own nervous system and because ownership increases compliance. Practice the breathing technique at bedtime as a normal routine. Do the five-four-three-two-one exercise in the car on the way home from school, not just when someone is panicking.

The brain learns what it practices. Regulation practiced in the calm becomes available in the storm. Regulation only encountered in the storm never gets fully learned.

The Three-Part Framework for the Moment

When your child is escalating and you are present for it, there is a simple three-part framework that gives you something to actually do:

Name it. "I can see you are really angry right now." Or frustrated, or scared, or overwhelmed, whatever is accurate. Name the feeling with specificity, without judgment, as a simple observation. This does the neurological work of emotion labeling we covered in Chapter One, it activates the prefrontal cortex and begins to bring the thinking brain back online, even slightly. It also communicates that you see them, which is itself regulating.

Claim it. "It is okay to feel angry. That feeling belongs to you." This step is about removing shame from the emotional experience. The feeling is not a problem. The feeling is real and valid. What happens next is where the choices live: but the feeling itself is allowed. Separating the emotion from the behavior is the core move of emotional intelligence, and this step is where you make that separation explicit.

Tame it. "What can we do to help that feeling get a little smaller?" Not "stop feeling that." Not "you need to calm down." An invitation, collaborative, curious, offering agency, to move toward regulation. If they have a toolkit, now is when you reference it: "Do you want to take some breaths? Do you need to move?" If they do not yet have a toolkit, this is where you offer options: "Should we get some cold water? Should we go for a quick walk?"

The framework works because it sequences correctly. It validates before it redirects. It names the emotion as legitimate before it addresses the behavior. It keeps the child's agency in the picture at every step. And it keeps you regulated: because you have something to do, a clear sequence to follow, which is itself organizing when you are standing in the middle of someone else's storm.

Temperament, and Why One Size Never Fits All

Here is something that parenting books rarely acknowledge plainly enough: children are born different from each other in ways that significantly affect how they experience and regulate emotion.

Temperament, the biologically-based, relatively stable pattern of emotional reactivity, sensitivity, adaptability, and intensity that a child brings into the world, is real, measurable, and not something you caused or can entirely change. Research by Stella Chess and Alexander Thomas identified nine distinct temperament dimensions, and their work established clearly that temperamental differences in children are present from birth and influence outcomes across childhood and beyond.

Some children are born with naturally high emotional reactivity, they experience feelings more intensely, they are knocked out of their window more easily, they require more time and support to return. This is not a defect. Some of the most empathetic, creative, perceptive, deeply feeling adults on the planet were highly reactive children who drove their parents to distraction and grew into extraordinary human beings.

Some children are born with naturally high sensory sensitivity, they are more affected by noise, light, texture, social stimulation, and the emotional atmosphere of the room. These children are not being dramatic when they melt down over the scratchy tag in their shirt. Their nervous system is genuinely registering that tag differently than your nervous system would.

Some children are naturally more adaptable, they transition between activities and emotional states with relative ease. Some are naturally slower to warm, requiring more transition time and more predictability before they can access their regulatory capacity.

Understanding your specific child's temperament profile, honestly, without judgment, without comparison to other children or to who you hoped they would be, is foundational to building a toolkit that actually works for them. A highly reactive, slow-to-adapt, sensory-sensitive child needs a fundamentally different approach than an easy-going, highly adaptable, sensory-neutral child. The principles are the same. The application has to fit the child.

The question that cuts through everything: what does regulation look like specifically for this child, in this body, with this nervous system? Answer that question and build from there.

Impulse Control: The Longest Build

Self-regulation and impulse control develop significantly between ages three and seven, continue developing substantially through adolescence, and do not reach full maturity until the mid-twenties when the prefrontal cortex finally completes its construction.

Read that again: mid-twenties.

This means that asking a sixteen-year-old to have the impulse control of an adult is asking them to operate hardware that does not yet fully exist. This is not an excuse for anything. It is an explanation that should inform your expectations, your interventions, and your patience.

The famous Stanford marshmallow experiments, in which four-year-olds who could delay eating one marshmallow immediately in order to receive two marshmallows later showed better outcomes on numerous measures years and decades later, captured something real about the downstream significance of impulse control and delayed gratification. Children who can tolerate the discomfort of waiting for a better outcome do, on average, show better life outcomes.

But subsequent research has significantly complicated the original findings. The ability to delay gratification is not simply a fixed trait of self-control that children either have or do not have. It is substantially influenced by environmental trust, by whether the child has learned, from experience, that the adults in their world follow through on promises. A child from an unpredictable environment who eats the marshmallow immediately may not be impulsive. They may be rational, making the sensible bet that the promised second marshmallow may not materialize because promised things often do not.

Impulse control builds on a foundation of felt safety. The child who trusts that the environment is predictable, that adults follow through, that the world is basically reliable: that child can tolerate the discomfort of waiting because they believe the wait will be honored.

Build the foundation of trust. Then build the skill of the pause on top of it. The pause, the gap between impulse and action, can be lengthened incrementally across years of patient practice. The three-year-old who takes one breath before grabbing the toy is doing the same neurological work as the adult who takes ten minutes before responding to a provocative email. The scale is different. The skill is the same. Acknowledge both as the genuine achievements they are.

ROOT THREE, REGULATE: The Pause At Each Stage

THE BUILDER (Ages 2–5): Impulse control at this stage is minimal and that is neurologically correct. The Builder's pause is measured in microseconds, not minutes. Your goal is not to teach them to delay their impulses: it is to be the external pause for them. "Stop. Let's take one breath before we do anything." You are the prefrontal cortex they don't have yet. Over thousands of assisted pauses, the skill begins to internalize. Celebrate every single one: "You took a breath before you grabbed it. That was so hard. I'm proud of you."

THE EXPLORER (Ages 6–10): The Explorer can begin to own the pause as a real, practiced skill. Teach it explicitly, in calm moments, with a fun framework: the traffic light (red, stop, yellow, think, green, go), the brain's "pause button," or whatever metaphor lands for your child. Practice it in low-stakes situations until it is automatic. The Explorer who has practiced the pause 200 times in low-stakes moments has a genuine chance of accessing it in a high-stakes one. The one who only ever encounters it during crises never will.

THE QUESTIONER (Ages 11–13): The Questioner's regulatory system is undergoing a second developmental upheaval: the brain is literally reorganizing, and impulsivity often spikes at 11–13 in ways that feel like regression. It is not. It is the Questioner's regulatory hardware being temporarily interrupted by construction. Maintain expectations while extending patience. The pause is now best framed as self-interest: "The thing you say in the next ten seconds can either solve this or make it five times worse.

Which do you want?" That frame actually reaches an 11-year-old brain.

THE ARCHITECT (Ages 14–17): The Architect's regulatory challenges are adult-scale, the stakes of impulsive decisions are real now, involving friendships, reputation, substances, relationships, and actions that can have lasting consequences. The most useful work at this stage is helping them develop their personal early-warning system: what does it feel like in your body right before you do something you'll regret? Building that self-awareness is the precondition for everything else. Regulation at this stage cannot be imposed, it has to be wanted. Connect it to outcomes they care about.

THE LAUNCHER (Ages 18–22): The prefrontal cortex finishes development in the mid-twenties, which means Launchers are still working with incomplete regulatory hardware in adult-consequence environments. This is genuinely difficult. The most helpful thing you can do is validate that difficulty while naming strategies that actually work in adult contexts: the 10-minute rule before sending an angry message, the sleep-on-it principle for big decisions, the trusted friend who provides an outside perspective. The pause is a lifelong practice. The Launcher is just beginning to own it as theirs.

Regulation is the skill that makes everything else accessible. Chapter Five explores what becomes possible once a child can pause: the capacity to step outside their own experience and genuinely enter someone else's. Empathy, real empathy, not performed empathy, is next.

TOOLS FOR CHAPTER FOUR

Build the Calm-Down Toolkit Together, The Right Way
Do this during a genuinely calm, connected moment, weekend morning, car ride, after a good dinner. Not after a meltdown. Start with curiosity: "I have been thinking about what might help you when you are really upset. Can we figure some things out together?" Work through each category: movement, breathing, sensory, connection, creative. Try at least one strategy from each category together in that calm moment so they have a real felt sense of what it does, not just a concept. Write or draw the toolkit on a card and post it somewhere both of you can see it. Update it as your child grows and as you discover what actually works versus what sounded good in theory.

The Daily Breathing Practice Pick one breathing technique, box breathing or the physiological sigh are the best starting points, and make it a daily family practice for thirty days, not as a behavior management tool but as a normal routine. Before bed. At the dinner table. In the car on the way to school. The brain learns what it practices, and practiced regulation becomes available under pressure in ways that regulation only encountered in crisis does not. Do it yourself, in front of them, every time.

The Co-Regulation Self-Assessment Before you engage with a dysregulated child, take a genuine ten-second inventory of your own state. Am I regulated right now? Is my breathing slow and deep or fast and shallow? Is my jaw tight? Are my shoulders up? If you are not regulated, take thirty seconds and actually regulate before you engage. The physiological sigh twice, deliberate slow breathing, a moment of physical grounding. The investment of thirty seconds returns enormous dividends because it changes everything about what comes next.

The Escalation Early-Warning Map In a calm moment, help your child identify and name their personal early warning signs, the physical signals that they are approaching the edge of their window before they go over it. Racing heart. Tight chest. Hot face.

Clenched fists. Voice getting louder. Thoughts speeding up. Create a family signal, a word or a gesture: that they can use to request a break when they notice the early warnings, before they are already over the edge. Then honor that signal every single time, without exception, without commentary. The signal only works if it always works.

The Temperament Conversation Spend some time, alone, with your partner if applicable, with genuine honesty, identifying your child's temperament profile. High reactivity? High sensory sensitivity? Slow to adapt? Needs connection or space when dysregulated? Does movement help or escalate? Answer these questions from observation, not from wishful thinking. Then redesign your approach to match the child you actually have rather than the regulatory toolkit that works for children in general. The child you actually have is the only one that matters.

CHAPTER FIVE

Empathy Isn't Soft: It's Strategic

The Five Roots this chapter develops: **CONNECT · NOTICE**

Here is a thing that gets said in corporate training rooms, family therapy offices, and leadership development seminars with such regularity that it has become almost invisible from repetition: empathy is important.

Yes. Fine. Agreed. Next slide.

What almost nobody explains, not with the specificity it deserves, is why empathy is important. Not in the abstract. Not in the "it makes you a nicer person" way that sounds good at a graduation speech and then evaporates in contact with actual life. In the concrete, measurable, this-specific-skill-produces-these-specific-outcomes way that would make anyone who understood it invest heavily in developing it.

So let us be specific.

Empathy is why some doctors get sued and others, with objectively similar outcomes, never do. Research by Wendy Levinson at the University of Toronto found that the single most significant differentiating factor between surgeons who got sued and surgeons who did not was not their technical skill, not their complication rate, not their expertise: it was whether patients felt heard. The doctors who got sued were perceived as dismissive, hurried, and uninterested in the patient's experience. The doctors who did not get sued were perceived as caring, attentive, and genuinely present. The malpractice data is a ledger of empathy deficits.

Empathy is why some negotiators consistently reach agreements that both parties find acceptable while others consistently reach impasses or agreements that fall apart. Research on negotiation effectiveness finds that the ability to accurately model what the other party needs, fears, and values, not just their stated position, but the interests and emotions underneath it, is one of the most powerful predictors of negotiation success. You cannot find the solution that works for both sides if you cannot genuinely understand what the other side actually needs.

Empathy is why some managers have teams with low turnover, high engagement, and strong performance while others have teams that are perpetually disengaged and quietly planning their exits. Study after study on workplace engagement finds that the primary driver of employee satisfaction is not compensation, not perks, not office environment: it is whether employees feel genuinely understood and valued by their direct manager. That feeling is produced almost entirely by whether the manager demonstrates real empathy.

Empathy is why some parents have teenagers who talk to them and others have teenagers who have concluded that talking to their parents is a waste of effort. The teenager who believes, from accumulated experience, that their parent will genuinely try to understand their experience before judging or advising it, that teenager talks. The one who has learned that conversations with parents produce immediate evaluation and unsolicited solutions, that teenager stops bringing things.

A woman named Sandra came to understand this when her sixteen-year-old daughter, Chloe, stopped talking to her. Not dramatically, there was no fight, no blowup, no moment Sandra could identify. Just a gradual quieting, a kind of closing down, until the conversations between them had been reduced to logistics. Rides, dinners, homework. Sandra thought Chloe was just being a teenager. Then Chloe mentioned, to her grandmother, who relayed it, that she had stopped telling her mom things because "she always tries to fix it, and I don't want it fixed, I just want her to listen." Sandra sat with that for a while. She started an experiment: she made herself wait until Chloe explicitly asked for advice before offering any. The first time Chloe brought something up, a friendship drama, complicated, Sandra said only, "That sounds really hard. What's the worst part of it?" Chloe talked for thirty minutes. At the end she said, "Thanks, Mom. That actually helped." Sandra had said almost nothing. She understood, finally, that she had been confusing being useful with being present. They were not the same thing.

Empathy is not weakness. Empathy is not softness. Empathy is not a luxury for people with abundant emotional resources who can afford to care about others' feelings.

Empathy is intelligence applied to people. It is the most useful social tool available to a human being operating in a world full of other human beings whose cooperation, trust, and goodwill are required for virtually every important outcome in life.

What Empathy Actually Is: Three Levels

Before we talk about building it, we need to be precise about what we are building: because empathy is not a single thing. Research has identified at least three distinct components that are often lumped together under the same word, and they develop somewhat differently and are relevant in different contexts.

Cognitive empathy is the ability to accurately understand what another person is thinking and feeling, to model their mental state, to see from their perspective, to comprehend what the world looks like from where they are standing. This is primarily an intellectual operation, though it draws on emotional experience.

Skilled negotiators, therapists, teachers, and leaders all rely heavily on cognitive empathy. You can have high cognitive empathy without feeling much yourself, some people with sociopathic tendencies actually have above-average cognitive empathy, which they use instrumentally. Cognitive empathy alone is necessary but not sufficient.

Affective empathy is the capacity to actually feel something in response to another person's emotional state, to be genuinely moved by their pain, to feel something of their joy, to have your own emotional system respond to theirs. This is the "climbing into the hole with them" dimension. It is what makes human connection feel like connection rather than transaction. Without any affective empathy, interactions feel cold and calculating. With too much, without adequate regulation, it produces emotional contagion, being overwhelmed by others' emotional states rather than being present for them.

Empathic concern, sometimes called compassionate empathy, is the combination: I understand what you are experiencing, I feel something in response to it, and I am motivated to help. This is the full expression of empathy that produces genuine prosocial behavior: the care that translates into action rather than stopping at understanding or feeling.

For children, all three dimensions develop and all three can be cultivated deliberately. The practical implication is that empathy-building is not just one thing: it involves developing the perspective-taking capacity (cognitive), the emotional responsiveness (affective), and the motivation to act on that understanding (concern). Different activities and practices develop different dimensions, and a comprehensive approach addresses all three.

The Sympathy Trap

Brené Brown's now-famous explanation of the difference between sympathy and empathy remains the clearest available, and it is worth sitting with for a moment because the distinction is not just semantic: it describes two fundamentally different relationships with another person's pain.

Sympathy looks at someone who is struggling and responds from above, from outside, from a comfortable distance. It says: that looks hard. I am sorry about that. I hope it gets better. Hang in there. The sympathy response is motivated, at least in part, by discomfort with the other person's distress: a desire to acknowledge it just enough to move past it, to offer something that closes the loop without requiring genuine immersion in the difficult experience.

Sympathy is not bad. It is appropriate in many contexts, particularly when you do not have a close relationship with the person who is struggling, or when the distance is necessary for your own functioning. Not every hard situation requires full empathic presence. Not every relationship warrants that depth of engagement.

But sympathy, offered in contexts where empathy is what is needed, produces a specific experience in the person receiving it: the feeling of being seen from a distance rather than genuinely met. The feeling that their pain is being managed rather than shared. The feeling of aloneness that persists despite the kind words, because kind words from outside the hole are not the same as someone inside the hole with you.

Empathy enters the experience. It says: I am here. I am not rushing you out of this. I can sit with you in it.

For children, particularly children who are struggling with something real, social rejection, academic failure, a loss of some kind, the ordinary heartbreaks of growing up, the difference between receiving sympathy and receiving empathy is the difference between feeling managed and feeling loved. The child who receives consistent genuine empathy from their parents develops the felt sense of being truly known, truly safe, truly accompanied through difficulty. That felt sense is the foundation of secure attachment. And secure attachment, as decades of research have confirmed, is one of the most powerful predictors of wellbeing across the entire lifespan.

The Neuroscience: Mirror Neurons and Shared Experience

In the 1990s, a team of Italian researchers led by Giacomo Rizzolatti discovered something surprising in their studies of macaque monkeys: certain neurons in the premotor cortex fired not only when the monkey performed an action, but also when the monkey watched another individual perform the same action. They called these mirror neurons, and subsequent research has identified analogous systems in the human brain.

The implications for empathy are significant. When you watch another person in pain, genuine pain, vividly depicted, many of the same neural regions that would activate if you were in pain yourself become active in your brain. You are not simply observing their experience and reasoning about it. You are, in a neurological sense, simulating it. Your brain is partially running the same program.

This is the biological substrate of empathy: the mechanism by which understanding another person's inner experience is not just an intellectual exercise but a genuinely felt, neurologically instantiated resonance. We are built for this. The capacity for empathic resonance is not something humans invented culturally. It is wired in.

But here is the crucial nuance: this capacity needs cultivation to develop fully, and it can be diminished by experiences that train the brain to deactivate empathic responses as a protective measure. Children who grow up in environments where attending to others' emotional states was dangerous, or where empathy was exploited, or where emotional attunement was simply never modeled or practiced, can develop functional deficits in empathic response: not because the hardware is not there, but because it was never fully activated and refined.

The good news: the hardware is there in virtually every child. Your job is activation and refinement, not installation.

Perspective-Taking: Building the Muscle Daily

Empathy's primary active skill is perspective-taking: the deliberate attempt to construct, from the inside, what another person's experience is like. Not to assume. Not to project your own experience onto them. To genuinely ask: from where they are standing, with what they know and feel and fear and need, what is this like?

This does not come naturally to young children. It genuinely cannot, neurologically, the prefrontal cortex regions that support theory of mind and perspective-taking are among the later-developing structures, and children under four or five do not yet have reliable access to them. The research on theory of mind development shows that the capacity to understand that other people have mental states different from one's own, beliefs, desires, knowledge, feelings, emerges around ages three to four and continues developing significantly through middle childhood and adolescence.

But once the hardware begins to come online, the software, the practiced habit of using it, is entirely a function of cultivation. And the opportunities to practice are woven into every ordinary day.

In conflict, before any problem-solving or consequence: "Before we figure out what happened, I want to hear what you think it was like for your friend. What do you think they were feeling when that happened?" This is not deflection from accountability: it is the prerequisite for genuine accountability. You cannot make meaningful amends to someone whose experience you have not genuinely tried to understand.

In observation, in the ordinary movements of daily life: "That cashier looked really exhausted. What do you think her day has been like?" "That kid at the park was playing by himself. What do you think was going on for him?" These brief, low-stakes observations build the habit of noticing other people's inner states as a normal feature of moving through the world.

In media, which children consume in enormous quantities and which is extraordinarily rich with perspective-taking material: "Why do you think that character did that? What were they feeling? What did they need that they weren't getting?" Fiction, on screen or on the page, presents emotional situations at one remove, which makes them easier to examine without the personal stakes that make real-life empathy harder.

In your own relationship with your child: "I have been pretty stressed this week. What do you think that has been like for me?" And then genuinely listening to their answer, receiving their attempt at perspective-taking, validating what they got right, gently correcting what they misread. This is advanced practice: it asks the child to apply perspective-taking to their own parent, which requires both emotional safety and genuine curiosity about another person's inner life.

Each of these is a small workout. None of them require significant time. All of them compound over years into a child who has made perspective-taking a reflexive habit rather than a deliberate effort.

The Fiction Prescription

One of the most consistently supported and most underutilized findings in the entire empathy research literature:

Reading literary fiction measurably increases empathy.

Not all reading. Specifically literary fiction: the kind that requires the reader to inhabit a character's inner life, follow their emotional and psychological arc across a narrative, and make sense of their motivations and choices from the inside.

Research by psychologists David Comer Kidd and Emanuele Castano published in Science found that participants who read literary fiction showed significantly higher scores on tests of theory of mind and empathy than participants who read popular genre fiction, nonfiction, or nothing. The effect was not small and it was consistent across multiple experiments.

The proposed mechanism is specific to what literary fiction demands of its reader. Genre fiction tends to present characters with relatively clear, externally legible psychology, the hero, the villain, the loyal friend, that requires little imaginative reconstruction on the reader's part. Literary fiction tends to present characters whose inner lives are complex, ambiguous, and revealed gradually and incompletely, requiring the reader to actively construct the character's experience rather than receive it. That active construction is perspective-taking. And perspective-taking practiced in fiction generalizes to perspective-taking in life.

What this means practically: reading to your children and with your children, and particularly discussing the inner lives of characters as you do, is not enrichment. It is not a nice extra. It is one of the most evidence-based empathy-development interventions available to you, requiring only time and books and a habit of asking the right questions.

Choose books with diverse characters, different backgrounds, different circumstances, different challenges than your child's. A child who only ever reads about characters who look, live, and experience the world as they do is not getting the full benefit. The empathic exercise that stretches the imagination most is precisely the one that requires inhabiting an experience genuinely different from one's own.

Ask the questions every time: Why do you think they felt that way? What would you have done in that situation? Have you ever felt anything like that? What do you think they needed? What do you wish someone had done for them?

These are not book club questions for adults. They are deliberate activation of the empathy system in a child's developing brain, through the most natural and enjoyable delivery mechanism available.

Empathy Is Not Agreement: The Critical Distinction

As children get older and begin to encounter genuine moral complexity, people who hold values different from their family's, situations where the right answer is unclear, conflicts where multiple perspectives are legitimate, one of the most important things to teach them is something that many adults never learn:

Understanding someone's perspective does not require agreeing with it.

This distinction matters enormously, and it gets confused constantly, in family conversations, in political discourse, in every domain where people with different views are trying to coexist. The confusion produces a false binary: either I agree with you, or I do not need to understand you. Either you are right, or your perspective is not worth inhabiting.

This binary makes genuine empathy impossible in exactly the contexts where it is most needed, across difference, across conflict, across genuine disagreement about things that matter.

The mature form of empathy holds two things simultaneously: I understand you and I do not agree with you. I can see why this situation looks the way it does from where you are standing, what experiences and values and fears are shaping your perception, and what it is like to inhabit your position, and I still reach a different conclusion than you do.

That is not weakness. It is not moral relativism. It does not mean that all views are equally valid or that genuine wrongs cannot be named. It means that understanding the person holding a view you find wrong is both possible and valuable, valuable because it is the only path to genuine engagement rather than mutual dismissal, and valuable because understanding how people arrive at harmful conclusions is the prerequisite for doing anything constructive about it.

Teaching children this distinction early, through discussions of conflict, through stories that present morally complex characters, through modeling it yourself when you speak about people you disagree with, is preparation for the world they are actually going to live in. A world that requires them to work alongside, live near, and occasionally collaborate with people whose worldviews differ significantly from their own.

Empathy does not mean everyone is right. It means everyone is human. That is a distinction with enormous practical and moral significance.

When Empathy Gets Hard: The Advanced Practice

Empathy is relatively straightforward, feels almost automatic, when directed toward people we love, people whose pain is familiar, people whose experiences resemble our own, people who have treated us well.

It becomes the genuine practice when directed toward people who have hurt us. Toward people whose values we find objectionable. Toward people whose choices we cannot understand or excuse. Toward people who are, in some meaningful sense, on the other side of a line from us.

This is where empathy either becomes a genuine character capacity or remains a situational skill deployed only where it is comfortable and withdrawn everywhere it is difficult. And the distinction between those two versions has enormous downstream consequences.

The parent who speaks about the neighbor they despise, the politician they find contemptible, the family member who has wronged them with pure contempt and zero curiosity, in front of their children, regularly, is teaching a specific lesson: empathy is for people like us. For people we agree with. For people who deserve it.

The parent who can say, genuinely, not performatively, “I strongly disagree with what that person did and I think it caused real harm. I also find myself wondering what their life has been like that led them there” is teaching something different and harder and far more useful: empathy is a practice that we apply even when it is uncomfortable, because understanding is not the same as excusing, and curiosity is not the same as approval.

This does not require becoming neutral about genuine wrongs. It does not require pretending that all positions are equally defensible. It requires only the willingness to ask, genuinely, what is it like to be that person?, before closing the judgment entirely.

That willingness, modeled consistently in front of children across years, produces adults who can engage with difference without defaulting to contempt. In a world that currently runs on contempt as its primary mode of disagreement, that is genuinely extraordinary.

Empathy and Emotional Contagion: Knowing the Difference

One important caution, particularly for highly sensitive children and for parents raising them: empathy and emotional contagion are not the same thing, and conflating them produces suffering rather than connection.

Emotional contagion is the unregulated absorption of another person's emotional state, catching their anxiety, their despair, their panic, their anger, and being swept away by it. A highly empathic child can walk into a room where something is wrong and immediately, involuntarily take on the emotional coloring of that room. They feel what others feel not as a deliberate practice but as an automatic and often overwhelming experience.

This is not a strength to be celebrated uncritically. For children who experience it intensely, it can be genuinely debilitating, making crowded environments overwhelming, making others' distress impossible to be near, making their own emotional regulation nearly impossible when others around them are activated.

Genuine empathy, mature, functional, sustainable empathy, includes the capacity to be present with another person's experience without losing one's own. To feel something in response to their pain without being demolished by it. To be moved without being swept away.

This regulation-alongside-empathy is a skill that takes time to develop, and it is one of the most important things highly sensitive children need help building. The message is not "stop feeling so much." The message is: your capacity to feel others' experience is a profound gift. Here is how to hold it without being held by it.

Teach them the difference between being present for someone and merging with them. Between empathic concern and emotional flooding. Between the open hand that can hold another person's experience and the open wound that has no boundaries.

ROOT FOUR, CONNECT: Empathy At Each Stage

THE BUILDER (Ages 2–5): Empathy begins as a reflex before it becomes a skill. Builders will sometimes spontaneously offer a toy to a crying peer or toddle over and pat someone who is hurt, that instinctive prosocial response is the seed. Your job is to notice and name it: "You saw she was sad and you went to help her. That was so kind." You are labeling the experience so it becomes conscious and repeatable. Also model empathy in action constantly, your responses to the Builder's distress are their first lesson in what it feels like to be understood.

THE EXPLORER (Ages 6–10): This is the prime window for deliberate empathy-building. The Explorer is in the middle of navigating complex peer relationships and actively needs the tools. Use books, movies, and real situations as constant empathy exercises: "What do you think she was feeling when that happened?" "Why do you think he did that?" "What would you have needed if that happened to you?" Make perspective-taking a normal, curious habit rather than a lesson. The Explorer who practices perspective-taking in fiction gets better at it in life.

THE QUESTIONER (Ages 11–13): Peer empathy becomes high-stakes at this stage, inclusion, exclusion, social cruelty, and loyalty are the daily landscape. The Questioner desperately needs empathy but is often drowning in their own emotional experience and has limited bandwidth for others'. This is not selfishness, it is self-preservation during a neurologically turbulent period. Work at the edges: the empathy conversation that happens about someone not in the room, the book character, the indirect approach. Direct "what is your friend feeling?" questions often bounce off a preoccupied Questioner.

THE ARCHITECT (Ages 14–17): The Architect is capable of sophisticated empathy and increasingly, in healthy development, begins applying it beyond their immediate friend group, to people unlike them, to abstract others, to causes and communities. This expansion is worth encouraging without overwhelming. "What do you think it's like to be in that situation?" directed at a news story, a book, a person they've mentioned, keeps the empathy muscle active. The Architect who develops cross-group empathy at this stage becomes an adult capable of genuine engagement across difference.

THE LAUNCHER (Ages 18–22): Empathy in the Launcher years becomes a professional and relational asset with direct, visible consequences. The Launcher who can accurately read their boss, their team, their partner, who can recognize when someone needs something they haven't explicitly asked for, is genuinely exceptional in environments that are largely populated by people who cannot do this. Frame it as the competitive advantage it actually is. And when they call you frustrated about a colleague or a relationship: model the empathy practice yourself. "What do you think is going on for them?" asked with genuine curiosity, not as a deflection.

Empathy without accountability is incomplete: a child can understand what someone else feels and still refuse to take responsibility for their role in causing it. Chapter Six closes that loop: owning what you did, without shame spiraling, and learning how to actually make it right.

TOOLS FOR CHAPTER FIVE

The Daily Perspective Question Once a day, at dinner, in the car, at bedtime, ask your child about one other person's experience. A friend they mentioned. A character in a show they watched. Someone they observed during the day. Keep it brief and conversational: "What do you think was going on for them?" Do not evaluate their answer. Receive it, build on it, add your own perspective. The habit of asking is the point, not the accuracy of any particular answer.

The Fiction Prescription, With Discussion Commit to regular reading together, books that feature characters whose experiences differ meaningfully from your child's. After reading, use these questions consistently: Why do you think they felt that way? What were they trying to get? What did they need that they weren't getting? What would you have done? Have you ever felt anything like that? These questions activate the empathy system directly and build the habit of looking for inner experience in characters, which transfers to looking for inner experience in real people.

The Hard Empathy Practice When you find yourself speaking negatively about someone in front of your child, a difficult person in your life, a public figure, a neighbor, pause and add the empathy dimension before closing the conversation. Not to excuse behavior you find genuinely wrong. To model the "I disagree and I wonder what their experience has been" form of mature empathy. Do this visibly, out loud, so the child can observe the practice in real time.

The Empathy vs. Agreement Conversation When your child dismisses someone entirely, "they're just wrong" or "I hate that person", introduce the distinction gently: "You do not have to agree with them. Can you tell me what you think it is like to be them right now? Just try to understand, not approve." Practice this regularly in low-stakes contexts so it is available in high-stakes ones.

The Post-Conflict Empathy Debrief After a peer conflict has cooled, not in the middle of it, after, revisit it from the other person's perspective. "Now that it is over, what do you think was going on for them? What do you think they needed?" Post-conflict is remarkably fertile ground for empathy development because the emotional activation has reduced, the cognitive bandwidth is available, and the child now has direct personal experience with a situation they can examine from multiple angles. Use it.

The Emotional Contagion Check For highly sensitive children: teach them the distinction between feeling with someone and being swept away by someone. "When you are with someone who is really upset, where do you feel it in your body? What does it feel like when you are empathizing versus when you are flooding?" Help them build the awareness to notice the difference, and develop strategies, brief physical grounding, conscious breathing, a moment of internal check-in, that let them stay present with others' experience without losing their own footing.

CHAPTER SIX

Own It: Accountability Without Shame

The Five Roots this chapter develops: **REPAIR · NAME**

Watch any political press conference following a scandal. Watch any corporate statement issued after something goes badly wrong. Watch two adults arguing about whose fault something is. Watch, if you can bear it, the comment section of any viral post about a public figure's bad behavior.

What you will observe, with striking consistency, is a species in full flight from accountability.

The non-apology apology. The passive voice deployed strategically to eliminate the subject from the sentence, "mistakes were made," "things happened," "it has come to light that", as though the events in question materialized from the ether without any human agency involved. The explanation that functions as justification. The immediate counter-accusation that redirects attention toward the other party's sins. The "I'm sorry you feel that way" that manages to apologize for the listener's emotional response while leaving the speaker's behavior entirely unaddressed.

We have developed, as a culture, extraordinary sophistication in the performance of accountability without the substance of it. We know what accountability is supposed to look like: the words, the tone, the appropriate facial expressions. We deploy the performance when social pressure demands it. And then, having satisfied the performance requirement, we return to the fundamental operating assumption that drove the original behavior: that owning a mistake is genuinely dangerous, that real accountability is for other people, and that the intelligent response to being wrong is to manage the perception of being wrong rather than to actually address it.

We learned this somewhere. Most of us learned it young. And we are teaching it, or failing to teach something better, every day to the children watching us.

This is the most countercultural chapter in this book. Because teaching a child to genuinely, cleanly, fully own their mistakes, without the asterisks and without the escape hatch, is swimming directly against the current of how our entire culture manages accountability.

It is also one of the greatest gifts you can possibly give them.

A father named Robert spent most of his son's childhood being, by his own description, a "blame deflector." Something would go wrong, a broken window, a hurtful comment, a mess, and Robert would immediately construct an explanation for why it wasn't quite his fault, or why the circumstances had been unfair, or why whoever was upset was overreacting. His son, Drew, absorbed this fluently. By fifteen, Drew could explain away anything. He had inherited his father's entire repertoire. The shift came when Robert attended a leadership training at work and the facilitator asked the group to think of someone they deeply respected, someone they would trust in a genuine crisis. Robert thought immediately of his old college friend, a man who had the specific quality of always owning his part cleanly and quickly. "He just never made you drag it out of him," Robert said. He went home that night and told Drew, then seventeen: "I've been teaching you the wrong thing about mistakes. I didn't do it on purpose, but I did do it. I want to try to show you something different." Drew was skeptical. Robert didn't blame him. He started in his own marriage, his own friendships, his own daily moments. Drew watched. It took about a year before Drew started doing it too, first small, then with real weight. Robert said it was the only parenting decision he'd made that he was certain had been worth it.

Why Accountability Is Actually Freedom

Start here, because this reframe matters and most people have never encountered it stated plainly:

Accountability is not punishment. Accountability is not weakness. Accountability is not the thing you are forced to do when you get caught and denial is no longer viable.

Accountability is freedom.

Consider what defending a version of yourself that is not real actually costs. The energy required to maintain a false narrative about what happened, to track who you told what, to manage the story, to stay vigilant against the details that contradict it, to deflect the conversations that might get too close to the truth. The relational distance that comes from knowing, somewhere beneath the defensiveness, that the people closest to you are relating to a performance rather than a person.

The research on this is consistent. June Price Tangney's decades of work on guilt, shame, and moral emotions at George Mason University finds that people who practice genuine accountability, who can own their mistakes cleanly and without excessive drama, report higher levels of self-respect, better quality relationships, less anxiety, and stronger performance over time. Not because they are more flawless than other people. Because they have eliminated the massive overhead cost of self-deception.

There is also a specific physiological component worth noting. The suppression of guilt and accountability, the active work of denying something you know you did, activates the stress response. Cortisol levels rise. Sleep quality decreases. The body is carrying the cognitive and emotional load of the unresolved truth.

The moment of genuine, complete accountability, "I did this, it was wrong, here is what I am going to do about it", produces, for most people, a measurable physiological relief. Not punishment. Relief.

Accountability is lighter than defensiveness. Always.

The Anatomy of a Real Apology

The English language contains four words that, in theory, accomplish everything accountability requires: I am sorry.

In practice, those four words have been so thoroughly deployed in so many contexts, with such varying degrees of sincerity, that they have lost much of their power. We say "I'm sorry" reflexively, habitually, as a social lubricant that smooths the moment without necessarily representing anything about the speaker's genuine understanding of what happened or genuine intention to change.

Children learn to say sorry the way they learn to say please and thank you, as a social performance, a word that ends a conflict and allows everyone to move forward. This is not meaningless. Social lubrication serves real functions. But it is not accountability, and conflating the two produces adults who believe they have taken accountability when they have only managed the surface.

A useful diagnostic: most apologies that fail to actually repair anything fail because they are missing one or more of five specific components. Understanding what those components are and why each one matters turns "saying sorry" from a ritual into an actual practice.

Specificity about what happened.

"I'm sorry for what happened" is not an apology. It is an acknowledgment that something occurred. It does not require the speaker to have understood what they did or why it was harmful.

It does not demonstrate awareness of impact. It is the minimum viable performance of contrition.

"I'm sorry I told your secret to Emma when you asked me to keep it. That was a betrayal of your trust" is an apology. It names the action. It names the harm. It demonstrates that the speaker has actually understood what they did, not just that a conflict occurred and needs resolution.

Specificity is uncomfortable. It requires the apologizer to say the thing out loud, to hear themselves describe what they did, which makes avoiding awareness of it much harder. This discomfort is the point. Accountability that costs nothing teaches nothing.

Complete ownership without qualification.

The word "but" is accountability's most reliable assassin. Everything before it gets erased. "I'm sorry I said that, but you really provoked me" is not an apology: it is a partial apology attached to a justification that relocates significant responsibility to the recipient. The person receiving it hears, accurately, that the apologizer has not actually taken ownership, because the "but" has distributed the blame.

"I was under a lot of stress" is not a mitigating factor in an accountability conversation: it is an explanation offered as an excuse. The stress may be real and relevant context for understanding why the behavior occurred. It is not relevant to whether the behavior was wrong and whether the apologizer owns it.

Complete ownership sounds like: "I did this. It was wrong. There is no version of the circumstances that made it okay." That does not mean the context is never discussable. It means the ownership comes first, unqualified, before anything else.

Acknowledgment of the specific impact.

Accountability without recognition of impact is incomplete. "I'm sorry I did that" addresses the action. "I'm sorry I did that, and I understand that it hurt you / embarrassed you / broke your trust /

made you feel unseen" addresses what the action actually did to the other person.

This step requires empathy: the perspective-taking capacity we developed in Chapter Five. You cannot genuinely acknowledge the impact of your actions on someone else without first genuinely trying to understand what their experience was. This is where the chapters connect: accountability done fully is built on empathy.

For children, this step can be taught explicitly: "After you tell them what you did, I want you to tell them what you think it was like for them. Try to describe their experience."

A concrete statement of what will change.

An apology without a commitment to change is an emotional transaction. It acknowledges the past without making any claim on the future. This is why the same apologies, issued repeatedly for the same behaviors, stop producing any meaningful response in the people receiving them, they have learned, from experience, that the apology is not connected to anything that will actually change.

"I will not do that again" is better than nothing. "Here is specifically what I am going to do differently when I am in that situation" is substantially better, because it demonstrates that the speaker has actually thought about the mechanism of change rather than simply intending an outcome.

For children: "What are you going to do differently next time you are in that situation?" is not a punishment question. It is a genuine inquiry into whether they have thought past the apology to the behavior change. If they cannot answer it, they have not yet fully processed the accountability.

Follow-through that proves the apology meant something.

This is not technically part of the apology. It is what happens afterward. And it is the only thing that gives apologies cumulative weight rather than making them noise.

An apology that is followed by the same behavior teaches something specific: words without follow-through are the currency of this relationship. An apology followed by genuine, observable behavior change teaches something different: when someone here says they are going to do differently, they mean it.

The follow-through is the proof. Without it, accountability is performance. With it, it becomes character.

The Fake Apology Hall of Fame

Because children will encounter all of these, and need to be able to recognize them, both in others and in themselves, it is worth naming them explicitly.

"I'm sorry you feel that way." This is perhaps the most sophisticated accountability evasion in common use. It appears to apologize while actually apologizing for nothing. The speaker expresses regret about the listener's emotional response, a response which, notably, the speaker did not cause, while the behavior that actually produced the response remains entirely unaddressed and unowned. This is not an apology. It is a polite dismissal.

"I'm sorry if anyone was offended." The conditional "if" does significant work here. It introduces the possibility that no one was actually offended, making the apology contingent on a condition that may not exist. It also relocates the problem to the people who experienced offense rather than to the behavior that caused it. Again: not an apology.

"I already apologized." Said with impatience, usually when the person who was hurt has not yet recovered from the hurt and the apologizer finds this inconvenient. The implicit message is that the social transaction of saying "I'm sorry" should have closed the account regardless of whether repair has actually occurred.

Whether the other person has healed is not relevant: the word was said.

"I'm sorry, but," We covered this. The "but" erases the apology and installs a defense in its place.

"What do you want me to do, grovel?" This one comes with a tone of injured dignity, as though being asked to genuinely account for one's behavior is an unreasonable imposition. It transforms the person seeking accountability into the aggressor and the person avoiding it into the victim of unreasonable demands. It is extraordinarily effective at shifting the emotional dynamic of the conversation away from accountability and toward resentment.

Teaching children to recognize these patterns, in stories, in public figures, eventually in themselves, is not cynicism. It is literacy. They need to know what accountability actually looks like in order to practice it, and they need to know what it does not look like in order to avoid the counterfeit versions that feel like accountability without doing any of the work.

Why Children Resist Accountability: The Full Picture

Some children arrive at accountability relatively easily. They mess up, they feel genuine guilt, they want to make it right, and with some support and structure they do. These children are a pleasure to parent through mistakes because the accountability instinct is already functional: it just needs direction.

And then there are the others.

The children who, when confronted with evidence of something they did wrong, escalate rather than soften. Who construct alternative explanations for what happened with impressive speed and creativity. Who manage to somehow become the injured party in conversations about their behavior. Who can look you directly in the eye and maintain a position you know to be false, with apparent complete conviction, and then be genuinely surprised when you are not persuaded.

Before labeling any of this as defiant, manipulative, or pathological: it is worth understanding what is almost certainly actually driving it.

The accountability environment has not been established. If the consistent experience in this home is that admitting a mistake produces explosion, extended lecture, character assassination, or lasting damage to the relationship: the child is not resisting accountability out of moral deficiency. They are avoiding a known hazard. This is rational self-preservation, and the solution is not to press harder but to change the environment. We covered this in Chapter Three.

Shame has been activated rather than guilt. A child who is in full shame, who has moved from "I did something wrong" to "I am wrong, I am defective, this is evidence about who I am as a person", cannot access accountability. They are in survival mode. The threat is not external. It is internal. And survival mode produces defense, not openness. The accountability conversation has to wait until the shame has reduced enough that the child can engage without feeling existentially threatened.

There is no template for what genuine accountability looks like. If a child has never watched an adult in their life own a mistake fully, cleanly, without drama and without the asterisks, accountability is an abstract concept, not a lived experience they can replicate. They know the word. They do not know the practice. This is a modeling failure, not a character failure, and it is fixable.

The resistance is protective, not callous. There is an important distinction between a child who resists accountability because admitting the mistake feels dangerous, and a child who resists accountability because they genuinely do not care that someone was hurt. The former is the vast majority of accountability resistance in children. The latter is less common and genuinely warrants more careful attention. But assume self-protection first. It is almost always right.

Building Accountability at Every Age

The accountability script looks different at different developmental stages, and expecting five-year-old accountability from a five-year-old and teenage-level accountability from a teenager requires calibrating to where the child actually is.

ROOT FIVE, REPAIR: Accountability At Each Stage

THE BUILDER (Ages 2–5): The goal is building the habit of repair, not sophisticated moral reasoning. Young children are not yet capable of the complex perspective-taking and impulse control that genuine accountability requires. What they can build is the physical and behavioral habit: we hurt people, we check on them, we say we are sorry, we try to fix it. The words "I'm sorry" matter less at this age than the behavior of turning toward the person who was hurt and doing something to address it. "Let's go see if she is okay" is more developmentally appropriate and more useful than an elaborate coached apology that means nothing to the child delivering it.

THE EXPLORER (Ages 6–10): Perspective-taking is now genuinely developing. Explorers can begin to understand that their actions had an impact on another person's inner experience, not just on the external situation. The accountability script becomes more meaningful: what did you do, how did it affect them, what can you do to make it better? Role-playing accountability scenarios in calm moments, not as punishment, but as skill-building, is remarkably effective at this age. Children who practice the script in low-stakes contexts have it available in high-stakes ones.

THE QUESTIONER (Ages 11–13): The Questioner can engage with accountability conceptually but is intensely vulnerable to shame activation at this stage. Identity is fragile and under construction. An admission of wrongdoing can feel like a verdict on who they are as a person. Keep the behavior-versus-identity distinction central and consistent: "What you did was wrong" is a very different sentence from "You are someone who does wrong things." Be patient with the first layer of defense: it is almost always self-protection, not callousness.

THE ARCHITECT (Ages 14–17): The Architect has the cognitive capacity for full, sophisticated accountability but the stakes are now real, reputation, relationships, trust. Accountability conversations at this stage require you to hear their perspective genuinely before insisting on yours. The Architect who feels understood, even in a moment of genuine wrongdoing, is far more capable of actual accountability than one who feels cornered. And when they do get it right, when they own something fully and it costs them something, recognize it explicitly. Voluntary accountability at 15 is extraordinary. Treat it that way.

THE LAUNCHER (Ages 18–22): Accountability in the Launcher years plays out in adult-consequence arenas: professional relationships, serious partnerships, financial commitments. The patterns installed in childhood are now running without you. Your role shifts to being someone they can call when they've made a significant mistake and need a trusted ear: not to rescue them from consequences, but to help them navigate accountability with dignity. "What do you think you need to do here?" is usually the right question. Let them find their own way to the answer.

Accountability Is Not Self-Punishment: The Perfectionism Trap

There is a specific population of children, and they are not uncommon, for whom the accountability lesson needs to be taught in a direction most parents do not anticipate.

These are the children who do not resist accountability. These are the children who, when they make a mistake, plunge directly into elaborate, extended, seemingly bottomless self-recrimination. Who cannot let it go. Who bring it up repeatedly, days or weeks after the incident has been addressed and repaired. Who say things about themselves, "I'm so stupid," "I'm the worst," "I always mess everything up", that are far more severe than anything the situation warrants.

These children are not practicing accountability. They are practicing self-punishment. And while it can look like accountability from the outside, they are certainly not defending themselves, it is functionally different in a way that matters enormously.

Genuine accountability has a cycle with a completion point: acknowledge, repair, learn, move forward. The movement is the key. Accountability is oriented toward the future, toward what changes, what is built back, what is learned.

Self-punishment is a loop with no exit. It circles the same ground repeatedly, not because it is processing anything or producing any change, but because the suffering itself has become the mechanism: the proof that the person cares enough, takes it seriously enough, is not a bad person because look how bad they feel.

For children who tend toward anxiety, perfectionism, or what psychologists call rumination, the repetitive, passive cycling of negative thoughts without moving toward resolution, the accountability lesson needs to explicitly include the completion. "I want you to take this seriously, and I also want you to know when the work is done. We acknowledged what happened. You apologized and it was accepted. You have thought about what you will do differently. That is the work, and the work is done. You do not have to keep feeling terrible about it."

Permission to move on, given explicitly, is something these children specifically need. Not permission to avoid accountability, permission to complete it.

Accountability is how we process what already went wrong. Chapter Seven zooms out to the bigger picture: what if mistakes weren't something to recover from, but something to mine? The debrief, one simple question asked consistently, changes a child's relationship with failure permanently.

TOOLS FOR CHAPTER SIX

The Accountability Script by Age Post this somewhere both of you can reference:

Ages 3–6: We hurt someone, we check on them, we say we are sorry, we try to fix it. Focus on the behavior of repair, not the words.

Ages 7–11: What did I do? How did it affect them? What can I do to make it right? What will I do differently? Practice in calm moments through role-play and low-stakes scenarios.

Teens: The full five-step framework. Emphasize behavior versus identity: what you did is not who you are. Practice the specific language of the commitment to change.

The Accountability Celebration When your child voluntarily owns something, particularly when it costs them something, when they could have gotten away with it, when the easier path was clearly available and they chose accountability anyway, make a genuine, visible deal of it. Not a performance. A real recognition: "That took real courage. I am proud of how you handled that. That is the kind of person I want to be raising." Intrinsic accountability is built when the child connects honesty with self-respect, not just with consequence management. Your recognition of their courage is a significant part of how that connection forms.

The Fake Apology Recognition Practice Over dinner or in the car, bring up examples of apologies from the news, from stories, from public figures, good ones and bad ones. Discuss them together: was that a real apology? What made it real or not real? What was missing? What would have made it more genuine? This is not cynicism training. It is accountability literacy, and it builds both recognition and vocabulary.

The Completion Practice For children who get stuck in self-punishment loops: establish an explicit completion ritual after an accountability cycle. When the acknowledgment has been made, the repair has happened, and the lesson has been extracted, name it out loud: "The work is done. You handled it. We are moving forward." The explicit permission to move on, given by a trusted adult, is sometimes exactly what these children need to break the loop.

The Repair Debrief After any meaningful accountability moment, once the emotional temperature has dropped and some time has passed, have a brief conversation: "How do you feel now that you handled it that way? What would it have felt like if you had denied it or blamed someone else instead?" This is not a reward system for good behavior. It is helping the child develop the intrinsic felt sense of accountability as relief, as integrity, as the version of themselves they actually want to be. The debrief connects the external behavior to the internal experience, and that connection is what makes accountability genuinely self-sustaining over time.

CHAPTER SEVEN

Mistakes Are the Curriculum

The Five Roots this chapter develops: **REPAIR · REGULATE**

There is a moment that happens in classrooms, in living rooms, on soccer fields, in music lessons, and at kitchen tables all across the country, multiple times every day, and its cumulative effect on children is enormous:

A child gets something wrong. And an adult responds.

The response takes maybe three seconds. Maybe ten. It is usually unremarkable, nobody photographs it or writes it down. The adult may not even remember it happened. But the child files it. Not consciously, not as an explicit lesson, as experience. As data about what mistakes mean, what they produce, what the appropriate response to them is, and what they say about the person who made them.

Multiply that three-second moment by the tens of thousands of times it occurs across a childhood, and you begin to understand why what we teach children about mistakes, not in lectures but in responses, may be one of the most consequential educational decisions we ever make.

Get it right, and you raise a child who treats their mistakes as information, who takes intelligent risks, who recovers from setbacks with speed and curiosity, who eventually runs their own internal debrief without needing you to prompt it.

Get it wrong, communicate, even inadvertently, that mistakes are evidence of inadequacy, that failure is something to be ashamed of, that the appropriate response to getting something wrong is to feel terrible about it or to hide it, and you raise a child who plays it safe to protect their ego, who avoids challenge because challenge means possible failure, who spends enormous cognitive and emotional energy defending a false picture of their own competence rather than building the real thing.

The three-second response. Over tens of thousands of repetitions.

That is the curriculum. Let us figure out how to teach it well.

What the Brain Actually Does With Mistakes

Before we talk about what to do, it helps to understand what the brain is actually doing when mistakes occur: because the neuroscience is both more interesting and more practically useful than most people know.

Your brain is, at the most fundamental level, a prediction machine. It is constantly generating predictions about what is going to happen next, in your environment, in your conversations, in the tasks you are performing, and comparing those predictions to what actually happens. When the prediction matches reality, the system notes the confirmation and moves on. When the prediction does not match reality, when something unexpected occurs, when the expected outcome does not materialize, when an error is made, the mismatch generates a specific kind of neural signal.

Researchers call this the error-related negativity, or ERN, a measurable electrical response first characterized by Michael Falkenstein and colleagues in the early 1990s that occurs in the brain within milliseconds of an error. Carol Dweck's subsequent research at Stanford University on mindset showed that how children interpret this signal, as a threat to their self-concept or as useful feedback, is one of the most consequential variables in their entire learning trajectory.

The fascinating part, and the part that changes how we think about teaching children to relate to mistakes, is what happens next. Neuroscientist Jason Moser and his colleagues at Michigan State found that what happens next depends enormously on what the person believes about their own intelligence and ability.

People who believe intelligence is malleable, that abilities can be developed, that effort matters, that mistakes are part of a process rather than evidence of a verdict, show a second brain signal following the ERN, a larger and more sustained response associated with the conscious processing of the error. Their brains, in measurable neurological terms, engage more thoroughly with mistakes. They attend to what went wrong. They extract information. They update their models. And they improve faster as a result.

People who believe intelligence is fixed, that you either have it or you do not, that effort is irrelevant because the underlying capacity is what it is, show little or no second signal. Their brains essentially disengage after the error flag. The mistake is not processed as information. It is processed as a verdict, confirmation of a limitation, evidence that should be minimized or defended against rather than examined. And they improve more slowly, if at all.

The belief shapes the neurology. The neurology drives the outcome.

And here is the part that should make every parent sit up straight: that belief, whether mistakes are information or verdicts, is learned. It is not fixed. It is built through thousands of micro-interactions with the adults who respond to a child's mistakes across years of development. It is built, in other words, by you.

A mother named Claire had not realized she was afraid of her daughter's failure until her daughter started refusing to try. Lily was nine, sharp, and had begun declining every activity where she wasn't already good. New sports, art classes, the science fair, all met with "I don't want to." Claire had thought she was being encouraging. She praised every success. She protected Lily from criticism. What she had inadvertently built was a child who understood, at some wordless level, that successes were celebrated and failures were problems to be managed. Safety meant staying inside what she already knew. One afternoon, Lily watched Claire attempt to hang a curtain rod, fail, attempt it differently, fail again, mutter "well that's interesting," try a third approach, and get it. Lily said, "You didn't get mad." Claire said, "Why would I? I just needed to figure it out." She saw something shift in Lily's face. She started narrating her own mistakes out loud after that, small ones, daily ones. "Oops, I miscalculated that. Let me try again." Nothing elaborate. Just modeling the relationship between mistakes and curiosity instead of mistakes and judgment. By the end of the school year, Lily had signed up for a pottery class. She was, by her own admission, terrible at it. She loved it.

The Mindset That Changes Everything

Carol Dweck's research on what she calls fixed and growth mindsets has been replicated extensively, applied across educational and organizational settings worldwide, and has held up remarkably well under scrutiny. It is worth understanding clearly because it is not primarily a theory about intelligence: it is a theory about how people relate to challenge, failure, and effort, and why those relationships matter so much.

The fixed mindset is a specific belief system: ability is essentially innate and static. You have a certain amount of intelligence, athletic talent, musical ability, social skill: a fixed quantity that effort can reveal but not substantially change. In this framework, challenge is threatening because failure under challenge means something about your fixed quantity. If you try hard and still fail, that is worse than not trying, because you have eliminated the explanation "I did not try" and the failure now reflects directly on capacity.

This is why fixed-mindset children often prefer easy tasks they know they can complete over challenging tasks where failure is possible. They are optimizing for the protection of their self-concept rather than for learning. And because learning requires challenge, requires working at the edge of current capacity, which means encountering failure regularly, they sacrifice growth to protect their story about themselves.

The growth mindset is the alternative belief system: ability is developed through effort, strategy, and learning from mistakes. Intelligence is not fixed. The brain is plastic. The skills and capacities you have today are not the ceiling, they are the current state of a process that continues as long as you keep working. In this framework, challenge is not threatening, it is the point. Failure is not a verdict: it is information about what needs to change.

These mindsets are not personality types that some people have and others do not. They are learned orientations, substantially influenced by the messages children receive from the adults in their lives. And the research on how they are transmitted is specific enough to be immediately actionable.

Praise for intelligence, "you are so smart", reliably nudges children toward fixed mindset. It communicates that the thing being praised is a fixed quality they possess. When they subsequently encounter failure, that fixed quality is now in question, and the rational response is to protect it, by avoiding challenge, by hiding mistakes, by looking for someone or something else to attribute the failure to.

Praise for effort and process, "you worked really hard on that," "I can see how much you practiced," "the way you kept trying different approaches was impressive", reliably nudges toward growth mindset. It communicates that the thing being praised is a behavior: a behavior they chose, can choose again, and that produces real outcomes. When they encounter failure, the response is: I need a different strategy, more practice, a different approach.

The shift in praise is small. The downstream difference is enormous.

The Three Types of Mistakes: A Full Framework

Not all mistakes are created equal. They do not all carry the same lessons, they do not all call for the same response, and treating them all the same, with either uniform criticism or uniform reassurance, misses the specificity that makes the teaching actually land.

Here is a framework that changes how both parents and children relate to errors, because it matches the response to what the mistake is actually about.

Careless mistakes are the ones that happen when we rush, when we are distracted, when we are doing something we know how to do but not with the attention the task requires. The important thing to understand about careless mistakes is that they are not about ability. The child who gets four math problems wrong because they rushed through the last five minutes of the test did not make math mistakes. They made attention mistakes. The lesson is not about math. It is about the relationship between attention and outcomes.

The right question: "You know how to do this. What got in the way?" Sometimes the answer is rushing. Sometimes it is distraction. Sometimes it is trying to do two things at once. The question opens a genuine investigation into what actually happened rather than producing a generic message about doing better.

Knowledge gap mistakes are the ones that happen because the person genuinely did not know something yet. These are the purest form of the learning signal: the brain's error flag firing in exactly the way it is designed to, flagging a gap between what was expected and what is known. The response to knowledge gap mistakes is simply: learning. The child who calculated the area incorrectly because they had not yet learned that formula made a completely appropriate mistake for someone at their current stage of knowledge. The response is to fill the gap, not to feel bad about having one.

The right message: "You did not know that yet. Now you do. That is the whole point of trying things before you have mastered them."

Brave mistakes are the ones that happen when someone attempts something at the edge of their current capacity, something genuinely hard, something where success was not guaranteed, something that required courage to attempt, and falls short. These are the mistakes that deserve not just acceptance but genuine, explicit celebration. Brave mistakes are the proof that growth is happening. You cannot make a brave mistake from inside your comfort zone. The attempt itself is the achievement.

The right response: "You tried something that was genuinely hard. It did not work out this time. That took courage. What did you learn?"

The child who internalizes this framework and can apply it to their own mistakes, who can identify what kind of mistake they made and match their response to it, is performing a level of metacognitive self-reflection that most adults have never been taught to do. They are not just experiencing mistakes. They are learning from them in a structured, efficient, self-directed way.

That is the goal. And it is fully teachable.

The Rescue Reflex: Loving Your Child Into Fragility

The uncomfortable truth that this chapter cannot avoid, and that every parent who reads it will recognize with some mixture of guilt and recognition:

When you rescue your child from the natural consequences of their mistakes, you are not protecting them. You are training them to believe they cannot handle difficulty without you. And that belief, absorbed quietly, over years of rescue, is one of the most significant obstacles to genuine resilience a child can carry into adult life.

The rescue reflex is not bad parenting. It is love, operating on instinct. When your child is struggling, when they are in pain, when something has gone wrong and you have the power to fix it: the drive to fix it is powerful and natural and comes from exactly the right place.

The problem is the message it delivers.

Every time homework gets hard and a parent does most of it for them, the child learns: I cannot handle academic difficulty alone. Every time a social situation goes sideways and a parent calls the other family to smooth it over, the child learns: I cannot navigate social conflict without adult intervention. Every time a consequence is coming and a parent intercepts it with the teacher or coach, the child learns: I am not capable of bearing the weight of my own choices. Every time a skill takes longer than expected and the bar gets quietly lowered, the child learns: when things are hard, the expected outcome adjusts rather than my effort increasing.

The accumulation of these rescues produces a child, and eventually an adult, who has been loved out of resilience.

Dr. Wendy Mogel, in her landmark book The Blessing of a Skinned Knee, makes the case powerfully: the greatest gift you can give your child is the experience of manageable difficulty without rescue. Not abandonment. Not indifference. Not letting them drown in something genuinely beyond their current capacity. The presence, the emotional support, the warmth, all of that can remain fully intact.

What changes is the solving. The solving stays with the child.

The child who struggles with the math problem for thirty frustrating minutes and then, finally, figures it out has learned two things. They have learned the math. They have also learned something far more important: I can handle difficulty. I can stay with something hard. I do not give up and I do not break. Hard things do not destroy me.

That second lesson, built through accumulated experiences of struggle and eventual success, is called self-efficacy. Psychologist Albert Bandura's research on self-efficacy showed it to be one of the most powerful predictors of outcomes across virtually every domain of human performance. People with high self-efficacy, the genuine, experience-based belief that they can handle challenges, attempt harder tasks, persist longer in the face of difficulty, recover more quickly from setbacks, and ultimately achieve more.

Self-efficacy cannot be given. It cannot be told. It is built only through direct experience of mastery, of encountering difficulty and navigating it, not because someone smoothed the path, but because you were capable.

Let them struggle. Stay close. Stay warm. Do not solve.

The struggling is the teaching. The solving robs the lesson.

The Praise Trap: How Good Intentions Go Wrong

Closely related to the rescue reflex is the praise trap: the instinct to protect children from the discomfort of failure by rushing in with reassurance that sidesteps the learning.

"Don't worry about it, it doesn't matter." "You'll do better next time." "That test wasn't fair anyway." "You're so talented, this is just a bad day."

Each of these responses is offered with love and with the genuine intention of reducing a child's distress. And each of them, by bypassing the mistake rather than examining it, communicates something the parent did not intend: this experience does not need to be understood. The appropriate response to failure is to feel better, not to learn something.

The child absorbs: mistakes are unpleasant things to escape from, not interesting things to examine.

Contrast those responses with: "That did not go the way you hoped. What do you think happened?"

This response does not rush past the disappointment. It does not pretend the outcome does not matter. It acknowledges the reality and opens toward genuine examination. It communicates that the mistake is interesting, that it contains information worth understanding, rather than simply being an obstacle to feeling okay again.

The child absorbs: mistakes are events that have explanations, and explanations lead to understanding, and understanding leads to something better.

The difference in those absorbed messages, accumulated across years, produces dramatically different adults.

The Debrief: One Question That Changes Everything

After any mistake, from the genuinely minor to the significantly consequential, there is one intervention that is more valuable than almost anything else you could do:

Ask: "What did you learn?"

Not as a rhetorical question. Not as a lecture disguised as a question. Not with the tone of someone who already has the answer and is waiting for the child to produce it. As a genuine inquiry. With real curiosity. As though the answer actually matters.

Because it does.

This question does several things simultaneously. It reframes the mistake as an event with extractable value rather than simply an experience to survive or forget. It keeps the brain in learning mode, the curious, engaged, processing mode, rather than shame mode. It communicates that what happened is interesting, not damning. And it puts the child in the role of the analyst rather than the defendant.

The debrief does not replace consequences where consequences are appropriate. A child who made a poor decision may still face the natural or logical consequences of that decision. The debrief happens alongside that, or after: not as a replacement for accountability but as the learning extraction that makes the mistake actually worth having had.

Over time, and this is the long game, the thing you are building across years and hundreds of small debriefs, children begin to ask the question themselves. Without prompting. After the failed test, after the friendship conflict, after the choice that did not work out: What did I learn?

When that question becomes internal and automatic, when the child has so thoroughly absorbed the debrief framework that they run it without needing you to initiate it, you have built something extraordinary. A self-directed learner who treats their own experience as a curriculum. A person who extracts value from difficulty as a matter of habit rather than exceptional effort.

That person does not fear failure. They use it.

That person is, genuinely, unstoppable.

Modeling Mistake-Friendliness: Your Role in This Chapter

Everything we have established about modeling in Chapter Two applies here with particular force, because children's relationship with their own mistakes is shaped profoundly by watching how the adults in their lives relate to theirs.

The parent who handles their own mistakes with defensiveness, self-punishment, or elaborate justification is modeling exactly that relationship. The parent who says "I got that wrong, here is what I am going to do about it, here is what I learned" is modeling something entirely different, and something their child will absorb and replicate, in ways they may never consciously connect to having watched their parent do it.

Share your mistakes. Not performatively: not manufactured mistakes offered as teaching moments that everyone can tell are not real. Real ones. The work project that did not go well and why. The conversation you handled poorly and what you wish you had done differently. The decision you made that in retrospect was clearly wrong.

The messier the better. A parent who only shares highly sanitized, long-past mistakes from which they have clearly and completely recovered is showing their child the acceptable face of failure. A parent who shares something real, something they are still processing, something genuinely uncomfortable, shows them that failure is part of ongoing life, not just history.

And then run the debrief on yourself. Out loud. In front of them. "What did I learn from that?" Let them watch you use the exact same question you are teaching them to ask.

ROOT FIVE, REPAIR: Mistakes As Curriculum At Each Stage

THE BUILDER (Ages 2–5): Builders cannot process the debrief verbally, "what did you learn?" lands as noise at age three. What they can absorb is your emotional response to their mistakes. Your calm, warm, unfazed reaction to a spilled cup, a broken toy, a failed attempt is the entire lesson at this stage. You are building their baseline emotional association with mistakes: is this a catastrophe, or is it just something that happened? Keep your tone matter-of-fact. Clean it up together. Move on without drama. That is the whole curriculum.

THE EXPLORER (Ages 6–10): This is when "what did you learn?" becomes available as a genuine practice. The Explorer has the cognitive capacity for basic reflection and is developmentally hungry for the sense of competence that comes from extracting meaning from experience. Make the debrief a light, casual, genuinely curious ritual rather than a formal sit-down. In the car on the way home from the game they lost: "What would you do differently next time?" Not with weight, with interest. Let their answer matter. Build on it. The habit forms through repetition, not through any single conversation.

THE QUESTIONER (Ages 11–13): Mistakes at this stage carry enormous social and identity weight, a public error in front of peers is genuinely mortifying in a way adults tend to underestimate. The debrief may need to happen much later, when the sting has reduced. Rushing the Questioner to extract lessons while the embarrassment is still acute backfires, you get defense, not reflection. "When you're ready to think about what you'd do differently, I'm interested to hear it" respects the timeline while keeping the channel open.

THE ARCHITECT (Ages 14–17): The Architect's mistakes have real consequences now, academic, social, sometimes legal or health-related. The debrief at this stage has to be co-equal: you are thinking through this together, not delivering a verdict from on high. "What do you think went wrong?" asked genuinely, followed by real listening, then your own honest perspective, that is the format. The Architect who experiences the debrief as a genuine collaborative inquiry, not a disguised lecture, builds the habit of self-examination that will serve them for decades.

THE LAUNCHER (Ages 18–22): The Launcher is running the debrief in adult arenas where the stakes are real and the feedback often comes from people other than you. Your role is to be a trusted sounding board for the debrief rather than the initiator of it. "So what are you taking away from that?", asked without judgment, after they've described a setback, is the most valuable thing you can offer. And sharing your own current mistakes, debriefed in real time: "Here's what I'm learning from something that went wrong for me recently..." models that the practice doesn't end at 22.

Mistakes between individuals don't just require personal accountability, they require navigation. Chapter Eight moves into the interpersonal arena: conflict, which most families treat as a problem to end, and what happens when you treat it as a classroom instead.

TOOLS FOR CHAPTER SEVEN

The Mistake Story, The Real Version Tell your child about a genuine mistake you made: not a minor embarrassment from long ago, but something real that had real consequences and produced real learning. Resist the urge to package it too neatly. Let it be somewhat uncomfortable to share. Children who see adults sit with the genuine discomfort of owning a real mistake learn something qualitatively different from children who see adults share polished retrospective wisdom. The discomfort is the lesson.

The Brave Mistake Dinner Ritual Once a week at dinner, each person shares one brave mistake from the week, something they tried that did not work out. No evaluation. No advice. Just acknowledgment and the one question: what did you learn? Start with yourself. Model what it looks and sounds like to share a brave mistake without shame and with genuine curiosity about what it revealed. The ritual, maintained over months and years, normalizes intelligent risk-taking as a family value.

The Rescue Audit, With Honesty For one week, track every time you intervene to prevent your child from experiencing the difficulty or consequence of a mistake. Write it down. At the end of the week, go through the list and ask, honestly, about each one: was that intervention necessary for safety or genuine wellbeing, or was it for me? Was I protecting them, or was I protecting myself from the discomfort of watching them struggle? The audit itself produces the awareness that changes behavior. Most parents are surprised by what they find.

The Praise Shift, Thirty Days For thirty days, practice catching outcome-focused praise before it leaves your mouth and redirecting to process praise. "You are so smart" becomes "you worked really hard on that." "You are such a natural" becomes "I can see how much you have practiced." "You are amazing" becomes "the way you stayed with that when it got hard was impressive." The shift will feel awkward at first. Track your success. Notice what changes in your child's response to challenge over the thirty days.

The Debrief Habit, Starting Now After any significant mistake or failure, yours or your child's, establish "what did you learn?" as the standard, expected, always-available follow-up question. No lecture before it. No lecture after it unless they have a specific question. Just the question, asked with genuine curiosity, and then listening to the answer as though it matters. Do this consistently enough and two things will happen: first, the child will start expecting it, and their brain will automatically begin moving toward the answer before you ask. Second, eventually, they will stop needing you to ask.

PART THREE: ADVANCED EQ

CHAPTER EIGHT

Conflict as a Classroom

The Five Roots this chapter develops: **CONNECT · REPAIR · REGULATE**

Think back to the first significant conflict you navigated as an adult: not a minor irritation, a real one. A relationship that went sideways. A workplace confrontation. A friendship that hit a wall. A family reckoning that had been building for years.

Now ask yourself honestly: who taught you how to handle it?

Not who gave you advice afterward. Not who helped you process it in retrospect. Who actually taught you, before it happened, the skills required to navigate it: the ability to stay regulated when things got heated, to listen to someone who was saying things you disagreed with, to express your own experience without attacking the other person, to find solutions that worked for both sides, to repair the relationship afterward?

For most people, the honest answer is: nobody. Or at least, not deliberately. Whatever conflict skills they have were assembled from fragments, watching how the adults around them handled it, absorbing cultural messages about what conflict is and what it means, surviving their own conflicts and extracting what lessons they could without much guidance.

The results of this haphazard, accidental education are visible everywhere. In marriages that end not because of catastrophic events but because small conflicts were handled badly for years until the relationship could not bear the weight. In workplaces where talented people cannot function on teams because they cannot navigate disagreement without escalating or withdrawing. In families where certain topics have been unmentionable for decades because nobody ever learned how to have the conversation, and the avoidance calcified into permanent distance.

Conflict is coming for your child. That is not pessimism: that is physics. Put two humans in any relationship of proximity and meaning, and eventually they will want different things simultaneously. They will have different needs, different perspectives, different thresholds for what is acceptable. They will disappoint each other, hurt each other, need things from each other that the other cannot provide, and disagree about things that matter.

The only question is whether they will have the skills to navigate it when it arrives.

Most people do not. Most people were never taught. Those people are your child's future colleagues, partners, friends, and neighbors. And in a culture that provides essentially no deliberate education in conflict navigation, teaching your child these skills is one of the highest-leverage investments you can make in their long-term wellbeing.

A couple named Derek and Vanessa had a rule in their house growing up, both of their houses, separately, before they met, that conflict was supposed to disappear. You either resolved it quietly and quickly or you stuffed it. What they discovered, ten years into their marriage, was that they had stuffed an enormous amount of things. They had two kids, ages seven and eleven, who were watching. Their older son, Marcus, had learned to freeze when anyone raised their voice. Their younger daughter, Sophie, had learned to escalate, if something was going to be a fight anyway, she would make it a big one and get it over with. Neither of them had been taught the middle way: that conflict can happen at normal volume, that you can disagree without the relationship cracking, and that you can actually come out the other side. Derek and Vanessa started doing something intentional: when they had a disagreement in front of the kids, they stayed in the room. They didn't perform a fight, but they didn't disappear into another room to manage it privately either. They let the kids see the frustration, and then the working through it, and then the resolution. Sophie stopped escalating. Marcus started using his words instead of going silent. Neither Derek nor Vanessa had said a single instructional thing. They had just stopped modeling that conflict was something to hide.

Conflict Is Not the Problem

The reframe that changes everything about how you talk about conflict with your children:

Conflict is not the enemy. Unresolved conflict is the enemy.

This distinction is not semantic. It is the entire foundation of healthy conflict navigation, and it is the opposite of what most children absorb from the culture around them.

The message most children receive about conflict, from family dynamics, from cultural narratives, from the way adults around them handle disagreements, is that conflict is dangerous, that its presence signals a problem with the relationship, and that the appropriate response is either to avoid it until it goes away or to win it as quickly as possible so it stops.

Neither of those responses produces good outcomes. Avoidance allows unaddressed issues to calcify into resentment, distance, and the slow erosion of intimacy that happens when people stop bringing themselves honestly to their relationships. Winning produces compliance or submission but not genuine resolution: the underlying disagreement is still there, now accompanied by feelings of defeat and often an undercurrent of resentment that will eventually resurface.

John Gottman's longitudinal research on relationships, spanning decades and thousands of couples and families, established something that has been consistently replicated: the presence of conflict does not predict relationship failure. The pattern of how conflict is handled does.

Families and couples who navigate conflict with curiosity rather than contempt, who address issues rather than avoiding them or escalating them endlessly, who repair quickly after ruptures, who treat disagreement as a normal feature of relationships between two distinct people rather than a threat to the relationship itself: these relationships are stronger, not weaker, for having navigated conflict well. The conflict reveals where the friction is. The navigation process either resolves it or deepens the mutual understanding that makes it tolerable.

Teach children, from the earliest age when they can understand it, that the goal is not conflict-free relationships. That is not a realistic or even desirable target. The goal is conflict-navigating relationships, relationships sturdy enough to hold disagreement, skillful enough to work through it, and connected enough to repair afterward.

That is the standard. Not the absence of conflict. The presence of skill.

The Gottman Four Horsemen: What Destroys Relationships in Conflict

If Gottman's research tells us that how conflict is handled matters more than whether it occurs, the natural next question is: what specifically does "handled badly" look like, and how do you teach children to recognize and avoid it?

Gottman identified four specific communication patterns, he called them the Four Horsemen of the Apocalypse for relationships, that are the most reliable predictors of relationship breakdown. They are not dramatic or unusual behaviors. They are patterns that show up in ordinary conflicts in ordinary families all the time, often without anyone recognizing them as the specific thing that is doing damage.

Criticism is the first and perhaps most common. Criticism attacks the person rather than the behavior. The surface content might be the same as a legitimate complaint, both a complaint and a criticism are about something that bothered you, but the direction is entirely different.

A complaint is: "I was really hurt when you shared my secret with Emma. I asked you to keep it private and you did not." It is specific. It is about the behavior. It describes the speaker's experience.

A criticism is: "You are so untrustworthy. You never keep anything to yourself. I cannot believe I thought I could tell you anything." It attacks the person's character. It generalizes from a specific behavior to a global identity statement. It tells the person not just that they did something wrong but that they are a certain kind of defective person.

Children who grow up in an environment where criticism is the default corrective tool learn two things: how to criticize others, and that being criticized means something about who you are as a person, which makes defensiveness and shame the automatic responses to any feedback. Both are catastrophic for long-term relationship health.

Contempt is the most destructive of the four by a significant margin. Contempt communicates superiority, disgust, and disrespect. It includes mockery, sarcasm wielded as a weapon, eye-rolling, sneering, and any communication that positions the speaker as fundamentally above the recipient. Gottman found that the presence of contempt in a relationship is one of the strongest single predictors of its dissolution, and that it is also, notably, one of the strongest predictors of the recipient getting sick, because chronic exposure to contempt is physiologically stressful in measurable ways.

The antidote to contempt is not just avoiding contemptuous behavior: it is actively building a culture of appreciation and respect that remains present even during disagreement. Relationships where people genuinely like and respect each other most of the time are far more resilient during the times they do not agree.

Defensiveness is the pattern of treating every criticism as an attack and responding to feedback with a counter-complaint rather than any acknowledgment of the other person's experience. "Well, you always do this" as a response to "I was hurt when you did that" is classic defensiveness. It dismisses the original concern and redirects the conversation toward the other person's faults. It is, at its core, a refusal to take any responsibility.

Children who have been raised in environments where accountability was consistently unsafe, where admitting any wrongdoing produced shame or punishment, often develop defensiveness as a protective reflex. The connection between Chapters Three and Six is direct here: the truth-safe environment and the accountability culture you build make defensiveness less necessary as a survival strategy.

Stonewalling is the shutdown: the withdrawal of engagement, the refusal to respond, the sudden and complete emotional unavailability. Stonewalling often follows flooding: the person's nervous system has been overwhelmed and the only available response is to stop participating in the interaction entirely. From the inside, it often feels like self-protection. From the outside, it feels like abandonment, and it is extraordinarily activating for the person being stonewall.

The important distinction here is between strategic stonewalling, using withdrawal as a punishment or a power move, and flooding-driven stonewalling, which is a physiological response to nervous system overwhelm rather than a deliberate choice. The first is genuinely harmful. The second is understandable but still needs addressing: the antidote is to recognize flooding early and ask explicitly for a break with a commitment to return: "I am getting too activated to have this conversation well right now. I need thirty minutes and then I want to come back to this."

Teaching children to name all four of these, to develop the vocabulary to say "I am being defensive right now" or "that felt contemptuous", gives them a tool to interrupt the patterns in real time rather than only being able to observe them retrospectively.

Positions vs. Needs: The Key That Unlocks Solutions

One of the most practically powerful concepts in conflict resolution, developed originally in the context of negotiation theory by Roger Fisher and William Ury in their landmark book Getting to Yes, is the distinction between positions and needs, sometimes called interests.

A position is what you say you want. A need is why you want it: the underlying interest, value, or concern that the position is trying to address.

Positions in conflict are often incompatible. Two siblings who both want the window seat on the airplane cannot both have it. Two children who both want the last piece of pizza cannot both eat it. Two adults who want fundamentally different things from a shared living situation cannot both get exactly what they described. When the conversation stays at the level of positions, conflict resolution becomes a zero-sum game, one person wins and one loses, or both lose in a compromise that leaves neither satisfied.

Needs, when you get to them, are frequently more compatible, and sometimes discoverable as not actually in competition at all.

The sibling who wants the window seat because they get motion-sick has a different underlying need than the sibling who wants it because they like to watch the scenery. One needs a specific orientation; one wants visual access to the outside. A solution that addresses both needs is available. It would never have been found if the conversation stayed at the level of "I want the window seat."

Teaching children to ask, and to genuinely want to know the answer to, "what do you actually need here?" is one of the most transformative conflict skills available. It shifts the frame from "how do we divide a fixed pie" to "what is each person actually trying to get, and can we find a way to address both?"

In practice, this sounds like: "I hear that you want to use the car on Saturday. What do you need it for?" "You are upset about the schedule change. What specifically about it is the problem for you?" "You keep coming back to this issue. What do you need that you are not getting?"

These questions are not manipulation. They are genuine curiosity about the underlying reality. And the answers almost always reveal more room to maneuver than the stated positions suggested.

Sibling Conflict: The Home Laboratory

If you have more than one child, you have accidentally constructed one of the most intensive and realistic conflict resolution training programs available to a human being. It is noisy and exhausting and occasionally involves significant property damage, and it is also genuinely invaluable.

Siblings are the perfect training ground for conflict skills because the conditions are maximally challenging in all the right ways. The relationship is permanent, you cannot opt out of your sibling the way you can opt out of a difficult friendship or a bad roommate. The stakes are real, these are people your child loves and is loved by, so the consequences of handling conflict badly actually matter.

The conflicts are constant and varied, everything from who ate the last yogurt to genuinely significant disputes about fairness, identity, and what it means to be seen and valued within the family.

Every conflict resolved well builds skill. Every conflict that escalates and then gets repaired teaches something about resilience. Every moment a child holds their position under pressure from a sibling who is also emotionally activated, every moment they manage to hear their sibling's perspective even when they strongly disagree, every moment they participate in repair after a genuine rupture, all of it is practice for the conflicts that will matter most in their adult life.

The parent's role in sibling conflict is one of the most important things to get right, because the wrong role actively undermines the skill-building that makes sibling conflict valuable.

The wrong role is referee: the parent as the authority who investigates, adjudicates, and delivers a verdict about who was right and who was wrong. Refereed conflicts do not develop conflict resolution skills in children. They develop the skill of presenting your case persuasively to an authority figure and waiting for external adjudication. This is occasionally a useful skill in life. It is not the one that matters most.

The right role is mediator: the parent as the process facilitator who helps both children express their experiences, ensures each one is genuinely heard, and supports them in finding a solution together. "I am not going to tell you who is right. I am going to help you figure out what you each need and whether we can find something that works for both of you."

This is harder. It takes longer. It will sometimes end in genuine stalemate where you do have to make a call. But practiced consistently, it builds in children the capacity to do this without you, to enter a conflict with a sibling or a friend or a partner and navigate toward resolution rather than waiting for someone with authority to fix it.

The Six-Step Conflict Resolution Framework

Give children a repeatable, learnable process for navigating conflict. Practiced in low-stakes situations when nothing significant is on the line, it becomes available, as an internalized pattern rather than a conscious checklist, in the high-stakes situations where it actually matters.

Step One: Pause and regulate. Nobody navigates conflict effectively while flooded. The first job is not resolution: it is regulation. Build in a mandatory cooling-down period as a family norm, not as punishment or shame but as simple practical strategy. Ten minutes for younger children. Thirty for teenagers and adults. The rule removes the stigma from needing time: you are not weak for needing to regulate. You are smart for knowing that flooded conversations do not produce good outcomes.

Step Two: Each person speaks without interruption. When the conversation begins, each person gets full, uninterrupted floor time to describe their experience, using "I" statements rather than accusations. "I felt hurt when you told Emma what I had shared privately with you, because I had specifically asked you to keep it between us" is a statement about a person's experience. "You are such a gossip and you never respect boundaries" is an attack. The rule about "I" statements is not just etiquette, it is a structural device that keeps the conversation oriented toward experience rather than accusation, which keeps the other person's nervous system less activated and their listening more available.

Step Three: The listener reflects back. Before anyone responds, they demonstrate that they received what was said. "What I hear you saying is that you felt betrayed when I shared that with Emma, because you had trusted me with something private." This step is enormously powerful and consistently skipped in most real-world conflicts. Its function is to slow the conversation down at precisely the point where it most needs slowing, to verify that actual communication has occurred rather than just a series of monologues, and to give the speaker the experience of being genuinely heard: which is itself significantly regulating.

Step Four: Identify underlying needs. Beneath the positions, what each person says they want, are needs. What does each person actually need from this situation? What value is at stake? What concern needs to be addressed? Finding the needs, rather than negotiating the positions, opens the space for solutions that neither party had initially considered.

Step Five: Brainstorm solutions together. Both people contribute options. The rule of the brainstorm phase is that no option is evaluated or rejected during the brainstorm, evaluation comes after. This rule exists because premature evaluation shuts down creative option-generation. Let all the ideas onto the table. Then evaluate together: which of these addresses both sets of needs?

Step Six: Agree and follow through, with a check-in. A solution only works if it is honored. State the agreement explicitly. And build in a check-in: "Let's see how this is working in a few days and adjust if we need to." The check-in removes the pressure of the solution being permanent and perfect: it is a working arrangement, subject to revision, which makes both parties more willing to commit to trying it.

Repair: The Practice That Makes Everything Else Work

Even well-navigated conflicts leave a mark. The conversation was difficult. Feelings were activated. Things were said, even skillfully, that landed hard. The relationship does not automatically return to its pre-conflict state once the immediate issue is resolved.

This is why repair is not optional. It is not an add-on to conflict resolution. It is the step that transforms a resolved conflict into a deepened relationship: the act of intentional reconnection after the rupture that communicates, more clearly than any resolution framework can: the relationship is bigger than this conflict.

Repair does not have to be elaborate. Sometimes it is a sentence: "That was hard. I am glad we worked through it." Sometimes it is physical: a hug, sitting together, a shared activity that re-establishes the normal comfortable texture of the relationship. Sometimes it is explicit: "I love you. I was really frustrated and I want you to know that the frustration was about the situation, not about you."

The message is consistent regardless of the form: we can fight and still be okay. I am still here. The rupture did not break us.

Children who receive this repair consistently, whose conflicts with parents and siblings are reliably followed by explicit reconnection, develop what attachment researchers call earned security. Mary Main's Adult Attachment Interview research at UC Berkeley documented this phenomenon: individuals who did not have secure early attachment but who later developed coherent narratives about those experiences, including the ruptures and repairs, showed attachment patterns indistinguishable from those who had secure attachment from the start. Repair, done consistently, is not just good for the relationship. It rewires the child's internal working model of relationships entirely.

Children who do not receive this repair learn the opposite: that conflict is genuinely dangerous, that it can break things permanently, that the appropriate response is either to avoid it entirely or to win it decisively enough that no repair is needed. They bring this learning into adult relationships, where it produces exactly the avoidance and escalation patterns we described at the start of this chapter.

Repair is the practice that makes everything else in this chapter worth doing. Build it into your family culture. Make it expected, normal, reliable. After every hard conversation, every significant conflict, every moment where something got heated, come back. Make sure the relationship is intact. Do it visibly, so your children see it and learn it and eventually do it themselves.

CONNECT + REPAIR + REGULATE: Conflict As Classroom At Each Stage

THE BUILDER (Ages 2–5): Conflict education at this stage is almost entirely observational and physical. Builders learn conflict by watching the adults around them handle it: the tone, the body language, the speed of escalation or de-escalation. Sibling conflict between Builders is best handled by narrating feelings, separating if needed, and modeling basic repair: "She was using that. Let's ask her if you can have a turn." You are the entire conflict resolution system right now. The Builder is watching how you do it.

THE EXPLORER (Ages 6–10): Sibling and peer conflict is the Explorer's primary training ground, and you are the best coach they will ever have, if you can resist being the referee. Practice the mediator role: "Tell me what happened. Now tell me what you needed. Now let's figure out what you both need." Explorers can genuinely learn the positions-versus-needs distinction at this age, and they are gratified by solutions they had a hand in creating. The conflict resolution script practiced hundreds of times in sibling disputes becomes the conflict resolution skill that serves them for life.

THE QUESTIONER (Ages 11–13): Peer conflict at this stage is seismic and often conducted at high velocity through digital channels, which amplifies everything. Your most valuable contribution is often not to help them win the conflict but to help them understand it: "What do you think was going on for them?" and "What did you actually need from that situation?" are more useful questions than "here's what you should have said." Also: model conflict resolution between you and your partner visibly. The Questioner who watches adults handle disagreement without catastrophe is getting rare and valuable exposure.

THE ARCHITECT (Ages 14–17): Parent-teen conflict is itself the curriculum at this stage. The arguments about curfews, privacy, and autonomy are the Architect's conflict resolution training. This means how you handle these conflicts matters as much as the outcome. Model the full framework on yourself: stay regulated, state your need rather than your position, acknowledge their perspective, look for solutions. They may not acknowledge it in the moment. They will remember it.

THE LAUNCHER (Ages 18–22): Conflict in the Launcher's world is now adult-scale, workplace politics, relationship ruptures, friendship fallouts with real stakes. Your role is sounding board and coach, not resolver. "What do you think they needed?" and "What does a good outcome look like for you?" are the questions to ask. Share your own adult conflict experiences honestly, not as instruction, but as parallel experience. The Launcher who knows their parent navigates conflict imperfectly but persistently has a model worth using.

Conflict is navigated between people. Chapter Nine zooms in on the boundary between them: the personal edge where your needs end and someone else's begin, and the skill of holding that line with confidence rather than guilt.

TOOLS FOR CHAPTER EIGHT

The Conflict Cool-Down Rule Establish this as an explicit, posted, consistently applied family norm: before any conflict resolution conversation, everyone involved gets a defined cool-down period. Ten minutes minimum for younger children, thirty for teenagers and adults. The rule is not a punishment and not a dismissal: it is a physiological reality: flooded brains do not navigate conflict well, and regulation is a prerequisite for resolution. Post the rule where everyone can see it. Apply it to yourself first and most visibly.

The Four Horsemen Vocabulary Teach your children, in age-appropriate language, to name the four patterns: criticism versus complaint, contempt, defensiveness, and stonewalling. Have the conversation during a calm family moment, not in the middle of a conflict. Use examples from stories and media rather than from real family conflicts. Then practice noticing: "That was a criticism, not a complaint. Can you try again with just the behavior?" Over time, children who can name the pattern can interrupt it.

The Mediator Role, Consistently The next time sibling conflict erupts, try the mediator approach instead of the referee approach. "I am not going to decide who is right. I am going to help you two figure out what each of you needs." Give each child full floor time. Reflect each position back. Ask about underlying needs. Guide toward a solution they generate together. This will take longer than just making a ruling. The skill development it produces is worth every extra minute.

The Positions-to-Needs Practice In low-stakes family decisions, where to go for dinner, what to do on a weekend, how to divide household tasks, practice the "what do you actually need here?" question. Get children used to articulating the underlying interest rather than just the stated preference. This builds the habit that transfers directly to conflict: the ability to move past what you said you want to what you actually need.

Post-Conflict Repair Ritual Build a consistent, reliable repair practice into your family culture. After any significant conflict, especially between parent and child, make the reconnection explicit. A brief check-in. A physical gesture if appropriate. An explicit statement that the relationship is intact. The content matters less than the consistency: the child needs to learn, through reliable experience, that repair always follows rupture in this family. That is the lesson that makes everything else in this chapter available.

CHAPTER NINE

Boundaries, Consent, and Saying No With Confidence

The Five Roots this chapter develops: **REGULATE · CONNECT**

Picture a child at a family gathering, maybe seven or eight years old, hanging back near the wall while a relative they barely know advances with arms open, expecting the hug. The child's body language is unmistakable: stiff, uncertain, reluctant. Their eyes slide toward their parent.

The parent, reading the social situation and not wanting to create awkwardness, says: "Go on, give Aunt Carol a hug."

The child complies. Aunt Carol is satisfied. The moment passes.

What was learned in that moment?

Not manners. Not respect for elders. Not the importance of family relationships. What was learned, absorbed quietly, without words, in the way that the deepest lessons always are, is this: when your body says no and an adult says yes, the adult wins. Other people's comfort with your physical person matters more than your discomfort with it. Your no, when it conflicts with a social expectation, is not valid.

Now multiply that lesson by the dozens or hundreds of times a version of it occurs across a childhood. Add in every "you're being rude" directed at a child who expressed an honest preference. Every "don't make a big deal out of it" in response to a child's discomfort. Every time a child's reluctance was overridden because the adults in the room valued smoothness over the child's actual experience.

By adulthood, the accumulated message is installed deeply: your no is a problem. Your needs are less important than the comfort of the people around you. The appropriate response to your own discomfort is to override it in service of harmony.

The research on where this leads is consistent and unsurprising. Dana Jack's work on silencing the self and subsequent research by Kristin Neff at the University of Texas on self-compassion and people-pleasing document the predictable patterns: chronic anxiety about disapproval, difficulty identifying what they actually want, relationships built on performance rather than genuine presence, resentment that accumulates invisibly until it surfaces in ways that seem disproportionate. And a persistent, gnawing sense of invisibility, of going through life being seen only in the approved version, never in the real one.

This chapter is about preventing that outcome. Not by raising children who are selfish or indifferent to others' needs, the goal is the opposite. It is about raising children who understand that genuine care for others requires genuine presence, and genuine presence requires genuine self-knowledge, and genuine self-knowledge requires the freedom to know, and to say: what is actually true for you.

Your no has value. Teaching your child to believe that about their own no may be one of the most protective things you ever do for them.

A mother named Grace had spent most of her own childhood being told she was "too sensitive" when she said no to physical affection. She had resolved to do something different, but when the moment came, her six-year-old son, Ben, pulling away from a goodbye hug from her own mother, she felt the old script rising. She opened her mouth to say "give Grandma a hug." She stopped. Instead she said, "Ben, do you want to give Grandma a hug, a high five, or a wave?" Her mother looked surprised. Ben considered for a moment and said, "High five." Grandma, to her credit, laughed and accepted it. On the drive home, Grace thought about what she had just done. She had given Ben the words for what he was feeling, reluctance, and made that feeling valid rather than overriding it. She had not made a political statement about bodily autonomy. She had just let him decide. He asked her later why she hadn't made him hug Grandma. She said, "Because your body belongs to you." He thought about this and said, "Does Grandma know that?" Grace laughed. "I think she does now," she said. He was satisfied with this. She was too.

What Boundaries Actually Are: And What They Are Not

The word "boundaries" has been somewhat flattened by overuse. It appears in self-help books, therapy offices, and social media posts with enough frequency that it has acquired a vague, therapeutic aura that makes it feel simultaneously important and somehow abstract.

The concrete version matters more than the abstract one about what boundaries are, because the concrete version is significantly more powerful and more teachable than the abstract one.

A boundary is not a wall. It is not a punishment. It is not a power move designed to control another person's behavior. It is not passive aggression dressed up in therapeutic language.

A boundary is information. Specifically, it is honest information about what is and is not acceptable to you, communicated clearly, to the people whose behavior is relevant.

When you say "I am not willing to be spoken to that way," you are not controlling the other person. You are telling them the truth about your limits. They can do with that truth what they choose. A boundary defines what you will do or not do, accept or not accept, engage with or not engage with. It does not, cannot, dictate what the other person does. It only describes your response to what they do.

This distinction matters enormously, and children who understand it are equipped to both set boundaries without guilt and receive others' boundaries without taking them as attacks. A person who sets a boundary with you is not controlling you. They are being honest about themselves. That honesty is a gift, even when it is uncomfortable to receive.

Boundaries are also not static. They are not rules handed down once and immutable. They are the living expression of a person's current needs, values, and capacity, and they change as the person changes, as the relationship changes, as circumstances change. Teaching children that their boundaries are theirs to define, and that they can update them as they learn more about themselves, is teaching them that self-knowledge is an ongoing process rather than a fixed set of answers.

Body Autonomy: The Foundation

Every conversation about boundaries begins with the body, and it begins earlier than most parents anticipate.

The body is the first and most concrete boundary, the most immediate and unambiguous territory that belongs entirely to one person. Teaching children that their body is theirs, that they have full authority over who touches it and how, and that their discomfort with physical contact is always valid and worth honoring, this is not just consent education in the narrow sense. It is the foundation of all boundary education.

The forced-hug scenario we opened with is the most commonly cited example, and it deserves the attention it gets. When a child is told to hug or kiss or sit on the lap of someone they do not want to hug or kiss or sit on, regardless of the reason, family expectation, social smoothness, the feelings of the adult involved, the message received is that their physical boundaries are negotiable when social pressure is sufficient. That their body is, in relevant circumstances, available for others to decide about.

No parent teaching this lesson intends it. Every parent teaching it is trying to navigate the real competing pressures of family relationships, social expectations, and a child who is doing something that reads as rude. These pressures are real. They do not change the lesson being taught.

The alternative is not abandoning family relationships or teaching children that they never have to do anything they find mildly uncomfortable. The alternative is a conversation that happens before the gathering, that establishes what is and is not required, and that offers genuine options: "You do not have to hug Grandma if you do not want to. You can wave, or give a high five, or just say hello. What feels okay to you?" The relationship is honored. The child's autonomy is also honored. And the child learns that the adults in their life take their physical comfort seriously: which is precisely the foundation they need to come to those same adults when something more serious than an unwanted hug occurs.

Because here is the downstream consequence that makes this worth the social awkwardness every single time: children who have been taught that their body belongs to them and that their no about their body is valid are significantly more likely to report unwanted touching, coercion, or abuse. They have the vocabulary and the permission. They have been shown, by the adults who love them, that their discomfort matters more than social smoothness. That belief, internalized early, is protective in ways that matter enormously.

The People-Pleasing Trap: When Helpfulness Becomes Self-Erasure

People-pleasing looks like a virtue from the outside. The people-pleasing child is cooperative, agreeable, helpful, low-conflict, and easy to manage. They do not make a fuss. They go along. They accommodate. From a certain angle, specifically the angle of an adult whose day is easier when children comply without friction, they look like a success story.

They are not. They are a warning sign.

People-pleasing is not kindness. Genuine kindness comes from an abundance, from someone who genuinely wants to give and is giving freely. People-pleasing comes from a deficit, from someone who has learned that their acceptance is conditional on their performance of agreeableness, and who is managing the ongoing anxiety of that condition by staying pre-emptively compliant.

The people-pleasing child has typically learned, through accumulated experience, one or more of the following: that their genuine preferences created conflict that felt dangerous; that expressing a contrary view produced disapproval from important adults; that the emotional climate of the home was more comfortable when they suppressed themselves; or that being genuinely seen, as a full person with actual needs and desires that sometimes conflict with others', was not safe.

They have learned to read the room with extraordinary sensitivity and adjust themselves accordingly. This sensitivity is genuinely impressive as a skill. It is also exhausting, alienating, and ultimately corrosive to the sense of self. A child who spends significant energy monitoring others' emotional states and calibrating their behavior to manage those states is not developing their own identity. They are developing a persona: an approved version of themselves that performs well under social evaluation.

In adult life, the people-pleasing pattern produces predictable and painful results. Relationships built on a performance rather than a person: where the other party has never actually met the real version. Chronic resentment at obligations that were never genuinely chosen but could never be declined. Difficulty identifying what they actually want, because wanting things for themselves has been so long suppressed that the signal is weak or absent. And an intimate acquaintance with the specific exhaustion of being useful while feeling fundamentally invisible.

The early warning signs are worth knowing: the child who always defers to others' preferences with no apparent investment of their own. The child who never expresses a contrary opinion in the presence of adults. The child who seems more attentive to your emotional state than to their own experience. The child who apologizes reflexively, for everything, including things that were not their fault.

These children are not easier to raise. They are asking, quietly, for something they have learned it is not safe to ask for directly.

Teaching the No: A Practical Curriculum

A confident, clean, guilt-free no is a skill: which means it is teachable, it requires practice, and it improves over time with the right conditions.

Here is how to build it deliberately.

Start by normalizing that no is acceptable. Not every no requires a reason. Not every no requires an apology. Not every no requires negotiation or qualification until the other person is satisfied. "No, I do not want to do that" is a complete sentence. "No, I am not comfortable with that" is a complete sentence. Children who have never heard an adult say no simply and directly, without elaborate justification, do not have a template for what that looks like. Provide the template.

Practice in explicitly low-stakes scenarios. The middle of a social conflict or a high-pressure situation is not where new skills are learned. Build the skill during calm, low-stakes moments when nothing significant is riding on the outcome. Role-play: "If a friend asks you to share your snack and you do not want to, what could you say?" Practice the words. Practice the tone, firm, calm, clear, not aggressive or apologetic. Practice staying with the no when the imaginary friend looks disappointed, because the discomfort of someone else's disappointment is exactly what most people-pleasers are trying to avoid, and practice is what builds the capacity to tolerate it.

Honor their no at home, consistently. Every time your child says no to something that is genuinely within their authority, a preference, a physical boundary, a reasonable limit on what they are willing to give, and you honor it, you are demonstrating that their no has power. That it works. That saying it does not destroy the relationship or produce punishment. Children who have experienced their no being consistently honored at home approach situations outside the home with the genuine, experience-based confidence that their no is real. Children who have only been told that their no matters but have not experienced it being honored have a concept, not a conviction.

Teach that a no can be kind. One of the most pervasive myths about saying no is that it is inherently unkind, that kindness requires always saying yes, always accommodating, always finding a way. This is both false and damaging. A clear no, delivered honestly and directly, is a service to both parties. It gives the other person accurate information. It prevents the resentment that builds when a yes is given that should have been a no. It models for everyone in the interaction that honesty about limits is a feature of healthy relationships, not a failure of generosity. "I cannot come to your event, but I hope it goes well" is kind. "I am not comfortable with that" is kind. Ambiguity in service of avoiding discomfort is not kindness, it is conflict deferred at the cost of integrity.

Model your own no, visibly and without drama. Say no in front of your children. Say it simply. Say it without the seven-sentence justification that implicitly communicates that a no requires an airtight case. "I am not available that evening, but thank you." "No, that does not work for me." Let them see that the no did not destroy the relationship, did not make you a bad person, did not require you to make the other party feel better about your limit. The model is the curriculum.

Consent: More Than a Safety Conversation

Consent education is often framed primarily as sexual safety education, critically important, but narrow. The concept of consent is actually foundational to all human interaction, and teaching it broadly from early childhood produces capacities that extend far beyond the specific safety context.

Consent is the genuine, informed, freely given agreement to an interaction. "Genuine" means not coerced. "Informed" means understanding what you are agreeing to. "Freely given" means that the person had a real option to say no and would not face unacceptable consequences for doing so.

Teaching this framework to children, in age-appropriate terms across development, builds several distinct capacities simultaneously.

It builds the habit of asking. "Do you want to play this game?" "Is it okay if I sit here?" "Can I give you a hug?" These questions communicate respect for the other person's autonomy. They model the practice of not assuming consent and instead seeking it. Children who grow up in families where asking is normal, where adults ask before touching, where preferences are checked rather than assumed, develop asking as their default mode of interaction. That default serves them well everywhere.

It builds the vocabulary for declining. Children need language for no, specific, practiced, available language that works across contexts. "I do not want to play that." "I am not comfortable with that." "Please stop." "No." These are learnable phrases, and they need to be practiced until they are available without requiring the child to compose them under social pressure in real time.

It builds the understanding that consent is ongoing. A yes at one point is not a permanent yes. A person who agreed to something yesterday can change their mind today. A person who said yes to one thing has not said yes to everything. This understanding, that consent is continuous and can be withdrawn, is one of the most important and most under-taught aspects of the concept, and it applies to friendships, activities, and commitments of every kind, not just physical interactions.

It builds the understanding that someone else's no is not a rejection. When another child says no to a game, a hug, a conversation, that no is not an attack on the child asking. It is honest information about the other child's current state. Teaching children to receive a no gracefully, without escalating, without taking it personally, without attempting to negotiate the person out of it, this is as important as teaching them to give a no. Both sides of the consent conversation matter.

Boundary Violations and What To Do About Them

Part of boundary education is preparing children for the reality that their limits will not always be respected, that people will sometimes push, pressure, ignore, or attempt to negotiate past a stated boundary, and giving them a framework for what to do when that happens.

The first thing to teach is recognition: a boundary violation is any situation in which someone continues an interaction after you have clearly communicated you do not want it. This can be physical, touching after you said stop, or verbal, continuing to pressure after you said no, or social, repeatedly asking after you have declined repeatedly.

The second thing to teach is that a boundary violation is not a reflection on the validity of the boundary. A violated no is still a valid no. The violation does not mean you were wrong to have the limit. It means the other person did not respect it, which is information about them, not about you.

The third thing to teach is graduated response. Not every boundary violation calls for the same intervention. A friend who keeps asking after you said no once may need only a clearer restatement: "I said no and I mean it." A situation that feels genuinely unsafe calls for more, removing yourself, involving a trusted adult, getting help. Children need to understand both that they have standing to respond to violations and that the appropriate response scales to the severity of what is happening.

And the fourth, perhaps most important, thing to teach is this: telling a trusted adult about a boundary violation is never the wrong choice. The child who has been taught that their limits matter, that violations are worth reporting, and that the adults in their life will take their report seriously, is the child who comes to you when something genuinely wrong is happening. That child is protected in ways that children who have been taught to manage boundary violations silently are not.

REGULATE + CONNECT: Boundaries and Consent At Each Stage

THE BUILDER (Ages 2–5): Body autonomy starts here, and it starts simply: no forced physical affection, full stop. "You don't have to hug Grandma if you don't want to. You can wave instead." Model asking before touching: "Can I pick you up?" This is not about formality: it is about installing the foundational message that their body belongs to them, at the age when that message goes deepest. Consent at this stage is also about teaching "stop" as a real and honored word in physical play: when they say stop, play stops, every time, with no exceptions.

THE EXPLORER (Ages 6–10): Explorers are ready for the full body autonomy framework and the explicit practice of both giving and receiving no. Role-play the scenarios: what do you say when a friend wants you to do something you don't want to? What do you do when someone keeps asking after you said no? The Explorer's social world is complex enough that these scenarios are real, not hypothetical. Also introduce the consent vocabulary: getting permission before touching, respecting others' no, understanding that a yes can change. These are learnable, practical, and urgently relevant to the playground they are navigating every day.

THE QUESTIONER (Ages 11–13): Social pressure is at its developmental peak at this stage, and the people-pleasing patterns that become entrenched here tend to persist. This is the critical window for explicit, ongoing work on the people-pleasing trap. Check in regularly: not invasively, conversationally: "Did you do that because you wanted to, or because you were worried what would happen if you didn't?" Build the habit of distinguishing genuine preference from anxious compliance. Also: digital consent matters now. What does it mean to share someone's photo without asking? What does it mean to screenshot a private conversation? These are the Questioner's consent questions.

THE ARCHITECT (Ages 14–17): Boundaries and consent at this stage are being tested in high-stakes contexts, physical relationships, party situations, social media dynamics, peer pressure about substances. The explicit conversations that feel uncomfortable to have are exactly the ones worth having. Build on everything you installed in the earlier stages. Name the dynamics: recognizing when someone is trying to negotiate past a no, recognizing when you are doing that to someone else. The Architect who can say a clear no in a charged social situation is drawing on years of practice. Make sure the practice happened.

THE LAUNCHER (Ages 18–22): Boundaries in the Launcher's world are adult-context: workplace limits, relationship expectations, the slow but crucial process of differentiating from family. The most important thing you can do at this stage is model healthy boundaries in your relationship with them: which means accepting their increased autonomy without treating it as rejection, respecting their right to information privacy, and not pressuring them to share more than they choose to. The parent who models good boundaries with their Launcher is teaching consent at the most advanced level available.

Knowing where your edges are is one thing. Knowing what drives you from the inside, what you actually care about when no one is watching and no reward is on offer, is another. Chapter Ten takes on the quiet crisis of external motivation, and what it takes to build the internal engine instead.

TOOLS FOR CHAPTER NINE

The Body Autonomy Policy, Explicit and Household-Wide Make it an explicit, discussed, named household norm: in this family, nobody has to hug, kiss, or be physically affectionate with anyone if they do not want to. This applies to children, to adults, to visitors, and to you. Discuss it proactively, not reactively, before the family gathering, not after the awkward moment. Children who grow up with this norm do not just follow a rule.

They internalize body autonomy as a value, which is a different and far more durable thing.

The No Practice, Low-Stakes and Regular Build regular, explicit no-practice into family life. Role-play scenarios: a friend pressuring you to do something you do not want to do, a relative asking for a hug, someone repeatedly asking after you have already declined. Practice the words, the tone, and specifically the skill of staying with the no when the other person looks disappointed. The practice is not theatrical: it is the genuine development of a capacity that requires repetition to become available under pressure.

The People-Pleasing Check-In Periodically and conversationally, not interrogatively, ask: "Did you do that because you wanted to, or because you were worried about what would happen if you did not?" This question, asked with genuine curiosity rather than judgment, builds the habit of distinguishing genuine desire from anxious compliance. Children who can identify the difference, who have developed enough self-awareness to know when they are acting from want versus from fear, have a significant advantage in building authentic relationships throughout their lives.

The Consent Conversation, Ongoing Make consent a running thread in family conversation rather than a one-time talk. When a child's no was respected at school, notice it. When a child navigated a boundary situation well, discuss it. When a news story or a book or a show features a consent-relevant situation, talk about it. The goal is to build a framework of vocabulary and thinking that is normal and familiar, not a set of crisis instructions for specific dangerous scenarios.

The Boundary Violation Response Plan Have an explicit, age-appropriate conversation: what do you do when someone does not respect your no? Practice the graduated response: restate clearly, remove yourself if needed, tell a trusted adult. Establish explicitly that coming to you about a boundary violation will never result in being in trouble and will always be taken seriously. Then follow through on that promise every time, including when the report is about a mild social situation rather than a serious safety concern. The child who has learned that their minor reports are taken seriously is the child who brings you the serious ones.

CHAPTER TEN

Intrinsic Motivation: Raising Kids Who Want To, Not Have To

The Five Roots this chapter develops: **REGULATE · NOTICE**

Picture a scenario most parents know well.

The reading log comes home from school. For every fifteen minutes your child reads, they earn a sticker. Enough stickers and they get a prize at the end of the month. Your child, who previously read for pleasure in bed every night, now reads exactly fifteen minutes. Then stops. Checks that you saw. Goes to do something else.

You have, without meaning to, done something fascinating and counterproductive to your child's relationship with reading. You have taken an activity they did because they loved it and reframed it as something they do to earn a reward. And the brain, which is quite good at updating its models, has updated accordingly.

Reading is now work. Work that pays. And when the sticker chart goes away at the end of the school year, the reading goes with it.

This is not a hypothetical. It is one of the most replicated findings in all of motivation psychology, and understanding it changes everything about how you approach the question of getting children to do what matters: not just now, when you are watching, but later, when you are not.

Two Kinds of Motivation, Two Completely Different Outcomes

There are, fundamentally, two engines that drive human behavior.

The first is external motivation: doing something because of what it will produce from the outside. A reward. Approval. The avoidance of punishment or disapproval. The presence of someone watching who will evaluate the outcome. External motivation is powerful, efficient, and reliable, right up until the external condition changes. Remove the reward, remove the observer, remove the threat, and the behavior that depended on them often disappears alongside them.

The second is internal motivation: doing something because of how it connects to something inside you. Because it is interesting. Because it matters. Because it is consistent with who you are and what you value. Because the doing of it is itself the reward. Internal motivation does not depend on external conditions. It is available in the absence of stickers, observers, and threats. It is the engine that operates when you are not in the room.

This distinction is not academic. It is the most practically significant insight in the entire motivation literature, with direct implications for how you raise a child who will eventually have to operate in a world that does not follow them around offering stickers.

External motivation produces compliance. It produces behavior that performs well under observation and measurement. It produces children who know how to optimize for the visible outcome.

Internal motivation produces character. It produces behavior that continues when no one is watching. It produces adults who do good work because doing good work matters to them, who maintain their values under social pressure because those values are genuinely theirs, who keep learning and growing after school is over because curiosity is intrinsic to who they are.

Both exist. Both have their place. The question is which one you are primarily building, and whether you are accidentally dismantling the internal kind while reaching for the external kind's short-term efficiency.

The Undermining Effect: How Rewards Backfire

In 1973, psychologist Mark Lepper and his colleagues at Stanford conducted an experiment that has been replicated so many times, in so many contexts, that it is now considered one of the most robust findings in psychology.

They gave preschool children access to drawing materials. The children who enjoyed drawing, who had demonstrated intrinsic interest in the activity, were divided into three groups. One group was told in advance they would receive a "Good Player Award" for drawing. One group received the same award as a surprise after drawing. One group received no award at all.

Two weeks later, the researchers reintroduced the drawing materials and observed how much the children chose to draw during free play.

The children who had received the expected reward, who had drawn in order to get the award, now drew significantly less than before the experiment. Their intrinsic interest in drawing had decreased. The children who received an unexpected reward and the children who received no reward showed no decrease.

The finding has been replicated across activities, ages, and cultural contexts: when you add a promised, expected external reward to a behavior that was already intrinsically motivated, the intrinsic motivation decreases. The external reward does not add to the internal motivation. It replaces it.

The mechanism is a shift in perceived causality. Before the reward, the child's internal explanation for why they are drawing is: I am drawing because I love drawing. After the promised reward, the explanation updates to: I am drawing because I get an award for drawing. And when the award goes away, the updated explanation no longer provides a reason to draw.

This is called the undermining effect, or the overjustification effect. And it is everywhere once you know to look for it.

The reading log that undermines the reader. The allowance that transforms household contribution into a transaction. The effusive praise for every drawing that gradually shifts the child's attention from the making to the evaluation. None of these are bad-faith interventions. All of them, deployed without understanding the mechanism, can do real damage to the intrinsic motivations they were meant to cultivate.

What This Does Not Mean

Before the preceding section produces a crisis about every star chart and gold sticker you have ever deployed, let us be precise about what the research actually says, and what it does not.

It does not say that all external rewards are harmful. It says that expected, promised, contingent rewards for already-intrinsically-motivated behavior undermine that motivation.

Unexpected rewards, a genuine, spontaneous "I am so glad you did that" rather than a scheduled reinforcement, do not show the same undermining effect. The child's internal explanation for why they did the thing is not disrupted by a reward they were not anticipating.

Rewards for behaviors the child has no intrinsic interest in, the homework they genuinely do not want to do, the vegetable they find genuinely repugnant, are not undermining anything. There is no pre-existing intrinsic motivation to undermine. External motivation is the only motivation available, and using it is reasonable.

Praise for effort and process rather than outcome does not show the same undermining effect as praise for ability or talent. "You worked really hard on that" is categorically different from "You are so talented." The first connects the child's self-concept to something they did: a behavior they chose and can choose again. The second connects their self-concept to a fixed quality they possess, which both creates fragility around that quality and subtly implies that the effort was less interesting than the natural gift.

The practical guidance that emerges: protect intrinsic motivation where it exists. Do not build reward systems around activities the child already loves. Watch for the shift from "I do this because I love it" to "I do this for the reward": it is visible in behavior and in the questions children start asking. And lean on unexpected, process-focused appreciation rather than expected, outcome-focused reward wherever possible.

A father named Ben noticed the shift with his daughter, Zoe, and almost missed the lesson in it. She had been drawing obsessively since she was four, filling notebooks, covering scrap paper, making art out of whatever surfaces were available. He had been proud, and he had started buying her art supplies, entering her drawings in the school fair, showing her work to relatives. Around age eight, something changed. She started asking, before starting any drawing: "Will you show people this one?" The drawing that followed was careful, deliberate, and, he thought, somehow less alive than the previous ones. The spontaneous art-making had slowed down. He didn't understand it immediately. He brought it up with her gently one afternoon. She said, "I don't want to make a bad one in front of everyone." He sat with that. He had turned her private joy into a performance. He stopped showing the work. He stopped commenting on it at all, mostly. He just kept the supplies full. Within a month she was filling notebooks again, messy, sprawling, unselfconscious. Nobody would ever see most of it. He thought that was exactly right.

Self-Determination Theory: The Three Ingredients

Psychologists Edward Deci and Richard Ryan spent decades developing what is now the most comprehensive and empirically supported framework for understanding human motivation: Self-Determination Theory. It identifies three core psychological needs whose satisfaction is essential for genuine intrinsic motivation to develop and thrive.

Competence is the need to feel effective, to experience yourself as capable of producing outcomes, as growing in skill, as genuinely able to handle the challenges you encounter. Competence is not the same as being perfect or always succeeding. It is the felt sense of growing mastery, of working at the edge of your current capacity and finding that you can push that edge. This is why challenge, calibrated to current ability, is essential for motivation: too easy and there is no sense of competence gained; too hard and competence feels unattainable. The sweet spot is stretch, tasks that require real effort and produce real growth.

Relatedness is the need to feel genuinely connected, to belong to relationships that are real and warm and mutual, to be seen and known by people who matter, to care about others and feel cared for in return. Motivation is not purely individual. It is profoundly social. Children who feel genuinely connected to their parents, their teachers, and their peers are more intrinsically motivated in the domains those relationships touch. The teacher-student relationship predicts academic motivation in ways that curriculum design and instructional method cannot fully explain. The parent-child relationship shapes motivation across every domain of the child's life. Relatedness is not a soft add-on to the motivation story. It is foundational.

Autonomy is the need to feel like the author of your own actions, to experience your choices as genuinely yours rather than coerced, controlled, or manipulated. This does not mean doing whatever you want with no constraints. It means that even within constraints, the experience of having made a real choice, for reasons that are genuinely yours, is available. Autonomy is the necessary condition for genuine intrinsic motivation, the thing that must be present for the other two needs to translate into self-directed, internally driven engagement.

Children who experience all three, who feel competent, connected, and autonomous in a domain, engage with that domain intrinsically. They do not need to be reminded, incentivized, or threatened. They want to.

Children who experience the absence of any one of these three needs in a domain tend toward external motivation or disengagement in that domain. The child who feels incompetent becomes avoidant. The child who feels disconnected from the teacher or subject becomes apathetic. The child who feels controlled, whose every choice is directed by external authority, becomes compliance-oriented at best and reactively defiant at worst.

Understanding which need is unmet gives you a specific intervention rather than a general puzzle about why a child is unmotivated.

Connecting Behavior to Values: The Long Game

The most durable, most robust, most genuinely autonomous form of motivation is values-based. It is the form that operates when external conditions change, when nobody is watching, when the stickers run out and the grade is already in and the consequences are distant or theoretical.

Values-based motivation requires that a person has actual values: not a list of stated commitments adopted because authority figures expect them, but genuine convictions about what matters and why, derived from their own experience and reflection.

Building those genuine values in children is a process that cannot be rushed or installed directly. It is built through the kind of conversations that the rest of this book has been enabling: conversations about feelings and why they matter, about empathy and what other people's experience is like, about accountability and what it actually means to make something right. It is built through the accumulated experience of being seen, known, and respected as a genuine person with a genuine inner life.

But it is also built through explicit, ongoing, curious conversations about values themselves.

Not lecturing. Discovering together.

"Why do you think honesty matters? Not why I think it matters, why do you think it does?"

"When you helped your friend today, how did it feel? Not what I hope it felt like: what did it actually feel like? Why do you think it felt that way?"

"What kind of person do you want to be known as, not famous, not impressive, genuinely known by the people closest to you as being what kind of person?"

These conversations do not produce immediate results. They are investments with long return horizons. But over years, they build something that cannot be built any other way: an internal moral architecture: a set of genuine convictions about what matters and why, owned by the child because they developed them, not because they were told to hold them.

An adolescent with a genuine internal moral architecture is not immune to peer pressure. That would be too much to ask of any developmental stage. But they have something to push back with when the pressure comes: a sense of who they are that belongs to them, not just the current collective opinion of the peer group.

That is what you are building with the values conversations. The payoff arrives when you need it most.

Autonomy Without Permissiveness: The Structure That Sets Children Free

One of the most persistent misunderstandings in parenting discussions is the equation of autonomy support with permissiveness: the idea that if you believe in children's need for autonomy, you must also believe in letting children do whatever they want with minimal guidance or structure.

This is wrong in both directions. Permissiveness does not actually support autonomy. It often undermines it, because genuine autonomy is not the absence of structure: it is the experience of making real choices within a structure that makes those choices meaningful.

A child who is told "you can do whatever you want" is not experiencing autonomy. They are experiencing overwhelm: the paralysis that comes from too many undifferentiated options and no framework for evaluating them. Real autonomy feels like: these are the real constraints, here are the real choices within them, your choice genuinely matters and has genuine consequences.

Structured autonomy looks like: "You need to practice your instrument for thirty minutes today. You can do it before school, right after, or after dinner, your choice." The outcome is required. The path is genuinely the child's to decide.

It looks like: "There is a consequence for what happened. I want you to help me figure out what a fair consequence would be." The accountability is required. The child's participation in designing it is real.

It looks like: "I have some concerns about this. I want to hear your thinking before I respond." The parental involvement is real. The child's perspective is genuinely sought and genuinely considered.

Age-appropriate autonomy expands the window of real choice as the child grows, in domains where the stakes are low enough to allow genuine experimentation and learning. The ten-year-old has more choice about their schedule, their activities, their friendships than the five-year-old. The teenager has more than the ten-year-old. The transfer of genuine agency is the developmental project of childhood, delivered incrementally in response to demonstrated capacity and in alignment with genuinely growing stakes.

The Identity Lever: Motivation's Most Powerful Form

In adolescence, the motivation landscape shifts dramatically. The authority of parents and teachers decreases as a source of motivational pull. The peer group rises. But beneath both of these is something that, if you have done the earlier work, is more powerful than either: identity.

Adolescence is, fundamentally, an identity project. Teenagers are engaged in the work of figuring out who they actually are, separate from their parents, separate from their childhood self, genuinely and distinctively their own person. This project is not optional and it is not a phase to be managed. It is the central developmental task of the period, and it consumes significant cognitive and emotional energy for good evolutionary reasons.

Parents who understand this can engage with it rather than fighting it. The most powerful motivational appeal available to a parent of a teenager is not consequence, not reward, not even relationship: it is identity. Connecting a choice to who the teenager wants to be.

Not as manipulation. Not as guilt. As a genuine invitation to self-consultation.

"Is that the kind of person you want to be?" asked with real curiosity, not with the tone of someone who already knows the answer and is waiting for the teenager to arrive at it, is an invitation to consult their own values rather than comply with yours.

"How does that fit with what you've told me you care about?" asked without sarcasm or agenda, is a question that takes the teenager's stated values seriously enough to hold them to them: which is itself a form of respect.

"When you look back on this in ten years, how do you think you'll feel about how you handled it?" is not a threat. It is an invitation to perspective-taking across time: a genuinely sophisticated cognitive operation that helps the present-focused adolescent brain access consequences that feel too distant to be motivationally real.

These questions work because they do not ask the teenager to comply with your values. They ask the teenager to consult their own. Which only works if you have spent years doing the work of helping them discover and articulate what those values actually are.

This is the payoff for the values conversations. This is where the long investment becomes available exactly when you need it most.

REGULATE + NOTICE: Intrinsic Motivation At Each Stage

THE BUILDER (Ages 2–5): Intrinsic motivation at this stage is almost entirely play-based, and play is not a break from learning, it is the primary mechanism of it. Protect free, unstructured play fiercely. Resist the urge to redirect, improve, or turn their play into an educational activity. The Builder who is allowed to follow their curiosity without constant adult intervention is building the intrinsic motivation template that will serve them for decades. Your job here is to protect the space, not fill it.

THE EXPLORER (Ages 6–10): This is the window to identify and invest in genuine interests, not activities you want them to have, but the things they actually light up about. Watch what they return to without being asked. Whatever it is, bugs, drawing, building, stories, music, numbers, take it seriously and invest in it. The Explorer who experiences deep intrinsic engagement in anything at this age has a lived template for what genuine motivation feels like, and that template is available for every other domain going forward.

THE QUESTIONER (Ages 11–13): The reward audit is critical at this stage, because well-meaning parents often inadvertently undermine the intrinsic motivation of activities the Questioner has genuinely loved. Check: is the sticker chart now attached to reading they loved? Is the allowance now attached to chores they did proudly? External rewards on already-loved behaviors are particularly dangerous at this age because the Questioner is simultaneously more aware of the transactional framing and more susceptible to having their identity as "someone who does this" eroded by it.

THE ARCHITECT (Ages 14–17): Autonomy is the primary motivational lever at this stage. Genuine choice, not manufactured choice, not choices between options you pre-selected, drives engagement in ways that nothing else can. The Architect who has genuine input into how they spend their time, how they learn, and what they pursue will outperform the controlled and directed Architect in almost every domain that actually matters long-term. Choose your battles. Grant autonomy wherever you honestly can. Reserve structure for the stakes that genuinely warrant it.

THE LAUNCHER (Ages 18–22): The Launcher is discovering which of their intrinsic motivations survive contact with real adult life and which ones were dependent on the structured environment of school and home. This is genuinely disorienting, many Launchers experience a motivation crisis in early adulthood as the external structure disappears. The values conversations you've been having for years are what they reach for in this vacuum. "What actually matters to you?" is not a rhetorical question at 20. It is the real and urgent question. Be available to explore it with them without providing the answer.

The internal engine needs to run in the world as it actually is: which increasingly means a digital world engineered to hijack it. Chapter Eleven is about raising children who can navigate that environment with their values and their attention intact.

TOOLS FOR CHAPTER TEN

The Undermining Effect Audit Look honestly at the reward systems you have in place. For each one, ask: is this for a behavior the child already intrinsically enjoys? If yes, consider whether the reward is building the behavior or eroding the intrinsic motivation behind it. You do not have to eliminate all rewards, you need to be strategic about which behaviors they are attached to and whether the short-term compliance gain is worth the long-term motivational cost.

The Values Conversation, Ongoing Over dinner, on a long drive, during a walk, ask your child: "What are three things that genuinely matter to you? Not what you think should matter. What actually does?" Do not argue or redirect. Receive the answer with genuine curiosity. Revisit the conversation every year or two and notice how the answers evolve. The ongoing practice of articulating values is itself values-building, the act of saying it out loud makes it more real and more owned.

The Autonomy Expansion Identify two or three areas of your child's life where you could offer more genuine, substantive autonomy: not false choices, but real agency over something that actually matters to them. Extend it. Observe what changes in their engagement, their initiative, and their sense of ownership. The data you get from watching a child exercise genuine autonomy is far more useful than anything you could learn from watching them comply under direction.

The Interest Inventory What does your child genuinely light up about, intrinsically, regardless of external reward or adult approval? Whatever it is, protect it. Invest in it. Find ways to connect it to other domains when genuinely possible. A child who experiences deep intrinsic engagement in anything has a template for experiencing deep engagement in other domains, and that template is worth more than any specific skill or knowledge they might acquire.

The Identity Mirror, For Teenagers When your teenager faces a decision with values relevance, try the identity question before the consequence conversation: "What kind of person do you want to be in this situation?" Not as a trap. As a genuine question asked with genuine curiosity. Then, and this is the difficult part, let them make the call. The experience of consulting their own values and acting on them, with you as a witness rather than a director, builds the identity-motivation connection that makes them self-directing rather than compliance-dependent.

CHAPTER ELEVEN

Raising Digital Humans

The Five Roots this chapter develops: **NOTICE · NAME · REGULATE · CONNECT · REPAIR**

Your child is growing up inside a technology experiment that has no control group.

There is no generation before theirs that navigated childhood with a supercomputer in their pocket, a social audience of hundreds available at all times, algorithmic content feeds designed by teams of engineers specifically to maximize engagement by exploiting the same emotional vulnerabilities this book has been teaching you to protect. There is no longitudinal data on what it does to a developing brain to spend a significant portion of childhood in an environment optimized not for the child's wellbeing but for the platform's engagement metrics.

We are running the experiment in real time. The children are the subjects.

This chapter is not about banning screens or declaring technology the enemy. That framing is both unrealistic and unhelpful. The digital world is the world your child is going to live, work, and love in. Competence in that world is not optional. Digital literacy is a genuine life skill, and children who are raised in technological ignorance or fear do not become safer or better adjusted, they become less equipped.

This is a chapter about raising children who can navigate the digital world with the same emotional intelligence they bring to every other domain of their lives, with self-awareness, with values, with the capacity to regulate their own behavior, and with the ability to recognize when a system is working on them rather than for them.

That is the goal. Not digital abstinence. Digital wisdom.

What the Platforms Are Actually Doing

To navigate something wisely, you need to understand its design. And the design of the major social and content platforms that most children spend significant time on is worth understanding clearly, because it is not aligned with your child's interests, or yours.

The business model of most major platforms is attention. Specifically, the conversion of user attention into advertising revenue. More time on platform equals more ad impressions equals more revenue. The incentive structure is therefore to maximize time on platform, to keep users engaged as long as possible, returning as frequently as possible.

To this end, these platforms employ significant engineering resources on what is sometimes called engagement optimization, the use of behavioral data, psychological research, and machine learning to identify and exploit the features of human psychology that most reliably produce continued engagement. Variable reward schedules, the same mechanism that makes slot machines compelling, are built into the core interaction loops: you do not know if the next scroll will produce something interesting, which keeps you scrolling. Social validation metrics, likes, comments, shares, are quantified and made visible in ways that directly target the social status anxiety that is particularly acute in adolescence.

Outrage and anxiety are more engaging than contentment. The algorithms know this. Content that produces high emotional arousal, fear, anger, social anxiety, moral outrage, generates more engagement signals than content that produces calm satisfaction.

The algorithm that optimizes for engagement will therefore systematically surface emotionally activating content over emotionally neutral content, regardless of what is true, healthy, or good for the person consuming it.

None of this is secret. Former employees of major platforms have described these mechanisms in significant detail in congressional testimony, journalistic investigations, and books. The platforms dispute some characterizations and adjust some practices in response to public pressure. The fundamental business model, attention for advertising revenue, has not changed.

Your child is the product, not the customer. Understanding this does not require paranoia. It requires clarity.

What the Research Actually Shows

The research on children, adolescents, and social media is complex enough that it is often misrepresented in both directions, either dismissed as inconclusive or weaponized for maximum alarm. The honest picture is more nuanced and more useful than either extreme.

Heavy social media use, defined in most research as several hours of daily active use, as distinct from passive or occasional use, is associated with increased rates of depression, anxiety, and loneliness in adolescents, with the associations being stronger for girls than boys and stronger for active social comparison use than passive consumption. Large-scale analyses of multiple national datasets find that the timing of the sharp increase in adolescent mental health crises in the United States and other countries closely tracks the widespread adoption of smartphones and image-heavy social platforms among teenagers in the early 2010s.

The associations are real. They are also correlational, not cleanly causal, adolescents who are already struggling may use social media more heavily, which complicates the direction of the relationship. The most careful researchers are explicit about this complexity.

What the research is clearest about: social comparison, the specific use of social media to evaluate one's own life, appearance, achievements, and social standing against others, is consistently associated with worse mental health outcomes. Passive scrolling, particularly of image-heavy content, is more consistently negative than active connection with specific people the user knows and cares about. Displacement of sleep by nighttime device use is associated with worse mental health outcomes through the sleep disruption mechanism, independent of content.

The picture that emerges is not "social media is uniformly harmful", genuine positive uses exist and are documented. It is more specific than that: certain patterns of use, in certain developmental windows, with certain kinds of content, are associated with measurable harm. The task is developing the specific wisdom to navigate those patterns rather than either avoiding the digital world wholesale or entering it without preparation.

The Specific Vulnerabilities of Adolescence

Understanding why the risks are higher for adolescents than for adults requires revisiting the developmental realities we have covered in previous chapters.

The adolescent brain is in the middle of significant remodeling. The prefrontal cortex, the seat of impulse control, long-term thinking, and the capacity to evaluate whether a behavior serves your actual interests, is still under construction. The limbic system, the reward and threat detection center, the seat of social sensitivity and emotional reactivity, is highly active. The result is a brain that is acutely sensitive to social signals, strongly motivated by peer approval, relatively poor at evaluating long-term consequences, and not yet well-equipped to regulate the emotional responses that social comparison and social exclusion reliably produce.

Now introduce that brain to a platform specifically engineered to exploit social sensitivity, deliver variable rewards through social validation metrics, and serve algorithmically-selected content calibrated to maximize emotional engagement.

The match between the adolescent brain's specific vulnerabilities and the platform's specific optimization targets is, to put it plainly, nearly perfect. The adolescent brain is precisely the brain that these systems affect most powerfully, and it is precisely the brain least equipped to recognize what is being done to it and choose differently.

This is not an argument for sheltering adolescents from all digital engagement. It is an argument for deliberate preparation, for giving adolescents the specific knowledge and skills they need to engage with systems that are, to use a phrase worth teaching them directly, designed to manipulate them.

Gaming: A Separate Conversation

Video games deserve their own treatment because they are often conflated with social media in parenting discussions, and the research picture, and the parenting approach, is meaningfully different.

The evidence on gaming is more mixed than the evidence on social media. Moderate gaming is not associated with the same mental health harms as heavy social media use, and some research finds genuine cognitive benefits, improved spatial reasoning, problem-solving, attention management, and even prosocial behavior in cooperative games. Games are not the enemy, and treating them as such typically produces either resentment or sneaky workarounds rather than genuine behavior change.

The specific concerns with gaming are narrower and more tractable: games are also explicitly designed using variable reward schedules and progression systems that are optimized for engagement rather than the player's wellbeing. The "just one more level" pull is engineered, not accidental. Multiplayer games introduce real social dynamics, cooperation, competition, trash-talk, exclusion, community, that can be genuinely positive or genuinely toxic depending on the game and the peer group. And heavy gaming can displace sleep, homework, physical activity, and in-person social time in ways that matter.

The practical framework: gaming is a legitimate activity that deserves the same kind of thoughtful engagement as any other. What are you playing? Who are you playing with? How do you feel when you stop? Are you choosing to play or feeling like you cannot stop? These questions, asked with genuine curiosity rather than as a prelude to a lecture, build the same self-monitoring capacity as the after-use check-in for social media.

The non-negotiable remains the same: devices out of the bedroom at night, and gaming does not displace sleep. Everything else is worth a real conversation before a rule.

What Digital Emotional Intelligence Actually Looks Like

The goal is not a child who avoids technology. It is a child who can use technology without being used by it. Here is what that looks like in practice.

They can identify when they are being manipulated. They know that the variable reward schedule of the feed is engineered to keep them scrolling. They know that the like counter is designed to produce social anxiety that drives continued engagement. They know that the algorithm surfaces content that makes them feel strong emotions because strong emotions drive clicks. This knowledge does not make them immune, knowing a magic trick's mechanism does not prevent the visual illusion. But it creates a slight gap between the pull and the compliance with the pull, which is exactly the pause we have been building throughout this book.

They can monitor their own emotional state during and after digital use. They notice when they have spent an hour on a platform and feel worse than when they started. They notice the specific feeling of social comparison anxiety: the particular flavor of inadequacy that comes from looking at curated images of other people's lives. They can name it. And because they can name it, they can choose to respond to it rather than just experience it. "I am comparing myself to people I do not know based on content they selected and filtered specifically to look impressive. That is what is happening right now."

They apply their values to digital behavior. The same standards of honesty, respect, and care for others that govern their face-to-face interactions also govern how they behave online. The keyboard does not create a moral exception. Text to someone you know is a real communication with a real person with real feelings. A comment section is a public space with real people reading it. Anonymity does not create permission. The question "would I say this to someone's face?" is not a perfect ethical guide, but it is a useful starting point.

They can exercise genuine self-regulation around use. They can decide to put the device down and actually put it down. They can recognize when use is serving them, connection, information, entertainment that genuinely refreshes, and when it is not. They can sit with the mild discomfort of not checking, which is itself a form of the self-regulation practice we built in Chapter Four.

They can come to you when something goes wrong. When they encounter something disturbing. When someone is unkind online. When they make a mistake in digital space, and they will.

The digital-world equivalent of the truth-safe environment we built in Chapter Three is the parent who responds to digital disclosures with curiosity rather than immediate consequence, who does not take the device as the first response to a reported problem, who has established clearly that bringing something hard to you is always better than managing it alone.

The Specific Conversations Worth Having

Digital wisdom does not develop automatically. It develops through the same mechanism as every other form of emotional intelligence in this book: repeated, honest, curious conversation over time.

The design conversation: How does this platform make money? What does it need from you in order to make that money? What is it doing to get what it needs? This conversation, had once with a ten-year-old and revisited as they get older and more capable of handling the complexity, builds the foundational media literacy that everything else depends on. You are not creating paranoia. You are creating informed engagement.

The comparison conversation: "When you look at other people's posts, how does it make you feel? Not what you think you should feel, what do you actually feel?" The specific discussion of social comparison, of what it is, why it is natural, why it is also not an accurate picture of reality, and why platforms specifically cultivate it, gives adolescents both vocabulary and permission to name what is happening to them rather than just experiencing it as mysterious inadequacy.

The identity conversation: "Who do you want to be online? Is that the same person you are in person?" The gap between the online persona and the genuine self is worth examining explicitly: not to eliminate all performance or curation, which is both normal and not inherently problematic, but to ensure the child is aware of the gap and can evaluate whether it is serving them or eroding them.

The mistake conversation, before the mistake: "Everyone makes digital mistakes eventually. When you do, not if, I want you to come to me. I promise my first response will not be to take your device. I want to understand what happened and help you navigate it." This conversation, had before the crisis, changes everything about whether the crisis gets disclosed.

The relationship conversation: "Is your digital life adding to your in-person relationships or replacing them? Are the people you spend the most time with online people you also spend real time with?" Not as an interrogation, as a genuine check-in about whether the digital social life is serving what human beings actually need from connection.

Sleep, Devices, and the Non-Negotiable

One recommendation in this entire chapter carries unusually strong evidence and deserves to be stated simply:

Devices out of the bedroom at night.

The research on adolescent sleep and device use is among the clearest in this entire area. Adolescents need significantly more sleep than adults, eight to ten hours, and are getting significantly less, and device use at night is a major contributor. The mechanism is dual: the blue light emitted by screens suppresses melatonin production and delays sleep onset, and the content itself, particularly social media and messaging, produces emotional arousal that further delays sleep.

Sleep deprivation in adolescents is associated with increased depression, anxiety, impaired emotional regulation, worse academic performance, impaired immune function, and higher rates of risk-taking behavior. The connection between adolescent mental health and sleep is one of the most robust findings in the literature.

Removing devices from the bedroom at night, charging them in a common area, for everyone in the family including parents, is the single highest-impact, most evidence-based digital intervention available to you. It is also one of the most contested, because adolescents experience it as significant, and it is. Hold the line. The evidence is not close.

A mother named Karen spent two years fighting her thirteen-year-old daughter, Maya, about phone use at night. The rules were established and violated repeatedly. The consequences were issued and absorbed. The conversations looped. What finally changed was not a new rule but a revelation. Karen sat down with Maya one weekend and, instead of issuing guidelines, said: "I want to understand what you're actually doing on your phone at night. Not to judge it, I genuinely want to know." What she heard was not what she expected. Maya wasn't watching videos. She was managing friendships in real time, a complex, anxious social ecosystem where going offline felt like abandonment, where not responding meant something, where the group chat never stopped. She was exhausted by it. She didn't know how to stop without social consequences. Karen realized she had been fighting the symptom. The actual problem was that her daughter had no off-ramp, no socially acceptable way to disconnect. They worked on it together: a group norm in the friend group about a 9pm cutoff, which two other parents helped establish. Maya didn't have to opt out alone. The phone went in the kitchen. She slept. Karen said the two years of fighting had been worth it, but only because the conversation they finally had was honest rather than prosecutorial.

Your Own Digital Behavior Is the Curriculum

Everything we established in Chapter Two about modeling applies here with particular force and particular awkwardness, because many parents are themselves navigating their own complicated relationship with the same platforms and the same pulls their children are navigating.

The parent who is on their phone throughout dinner and then has a conversation about healthy technology use is not being hypocritical in bad faith. They are caught in the same engineered pull their child is caught in. But the child sees it, and what they see is: this behavior is what adults actually do, regardless of what they say.

Your own digital habits are visible. Your reflexive phone-checking in the middle of conversations. Your scrolling before bed. Your emotional reactions to online content. The degree to which you are present or absent during family time because a device has your attention.

This is not a guilt trip. It is an invitation to the same self-reflection you are building in your child. What is your relationship with your own devices? Is it the relationship you would choose, deliberately? Are you modeling what you want them to learn?

The family that has an honest, curious conversation about everyone's digital habits, including the parents', is doing something qualitatively different from the family that applies rules downward to children while adults exempt themselves. The first conversation produces shared wisdom. The second produces resentment and the reasonable perception that the rules are about control rather than genuine concern.

NOTICE + NAME + REGULATE + CONNECT + REPAIR: Digital Wisdom At Each Stage

THE BUILDER (Ages 2–5): Screens are not developmentally appropriate as a primary activity at this age, and the digital parenting conversation here is almost entirely about your own behavior. Builders learn from what they see, and what they see is you with your phone. Put it down during the time you are present with them. Not always, that is not the standard, but deliberately enough that they experience you as genuinely present, genuinely here. The most important digital habit at this stage is yours.

THE EXPLORER (Ages 6–10): This is the stage to introduce the design conversation in simple terms: "Do you know how a video platform makes money?" Explorers are intensely curious about how things work, and platform mechanics are genuinely interesting to them when explained clearly. Start building the media literacy framework now, while they are young enough to find it fascinating rather than defensive. Also establish the after-use check-in as a family habit: "How do you feel now compared to before you started?" The habit of noticing is the beginning of all self-regulation.

THE QUESTIONER (Ages 11–13): This is the highest-risk window for social media harm, and it often coincides with first smartphone access. If you can delay social media access until 14, the research strongly supports doing so. If you cannot or will not, the comparison conversation is the most critical tool: "When you look at other people's posts, what happens inside you?" Name social comparison explicitly: what it is, why the platform cultivates it, why it is not an accurate picture of anyone's real life. The Questioner who can name the mechanism has some protection. The one who can only feel it has none.

THE ARCHITECT (Ages 14–17): The Architect's digital life is social life, separating them is neither possible nor desirable. The goal is not restriction but wisdom: the after-use check-in, the identity conversation ("is who you are online who you actually are?"), the recognition of the manipulation that the algorithm is performing on them. The no-devices-in-bedroom policy is most critical and most contested at this stage. Hold it. The sleep evidence is unambiguous. The Architect who sleeps is measurably better at emotional regulation than the Architect who does not.

THE LAUNCHER (Ages 18–22): The Launcher is now making their own digital choices in an environment with no parental oversight. Your influence is now entirely through what you modeled and what you built in the earlier stages. What does help: sharing your own ongoing relationship with your devices honestly, "I have been trying to be more intentional about my phone use and here's what I've noticed", as a peer-level conversation rather than a lesson. And staying genuinely available when digital situations go sideways, as they will, with the curiosity and lack of catastrophizing you promised them when they were twelve.

Eleven chapters of building. Chapter Twelve is the portrait: what a person looks like when all five roots are deep, when the work across childhood actually worked. It is also about the hardest part of parenthood: letting go.

TOOLS FOR CHAPTER ELEVEN

The Platform Design Conversation Sit down with your child, at whatever age they start using social platforms, and revisit periodically, and work through the business model together. How does this platform make money? What does it need you to do in order to make that? What does it do to get you to do that? This is not a fear conversation. It is a literacy conversation. Children who understand the design are not immune to it, but they have a tool that children who do not understand it completely lack.

The After-Use Check-In Establish a brief, consistent family habit: after significant device use, a quick check-in. "How do you feel right now compared to before you started?" No evaluation of the answer. Just the practice of noticing. Over time, children develop the habit of monitoring their own emotional state during and after digital use, which is the foundation of self-regulated engagement.

The Device-Free Zones, By Agreement Establish two or three device-free zones or times as family norms, dinner, certain weekend activities, the hour before bed, and apply them to everyone, including adults. Not as punishment. As a family value: in this family, there are times when we are fully present with each other. The norm works because it applies uniformly and because everyone participates in setting it.

The No-Device Bedroom Policy Make this non-negotiable and apply it to everyone. Devices charge in a common area. This is the single highest-evidence intervention in the entire digital parenting space, and it is worth the resistance it will produce. Establish it as a health practice rather than a punishment: we all sleep better without devices in the bedroom, and sleep matters.

The Preemptive Disclosure Conversation Have this conversation explicitly, before any crisis occurs: "When you make a digital mistake, and everyone does eventually, I want you to come to me. My first response will not be to take your phone. I want to understand what happened and help you figure out what to do." Repeat this conversation periodically so it stays fresh. The child who knows this policy exists in advance is far more likely to disclose when the time comes.

PART FOUR: THE LONG GAME

CHAPTER TWELVE

What a High-EQ Adult Actually Looks Like

The Five Roots this chapter develops: **NOTICE · NAME · REGULATE · CONNECT · REPAIR**

We have been building toward something. Not a perfect child. Not a child who never struggles, never fails, never makes choices that make you want to put your head through a wall.

We have been building toward a capable adult. A person who can feel deeply without being destroyed by it. Who can fail without falling apart. Who can love honestly, work with integrity, and navigate the genuine complexity of an actual human life with skill, resilience, and something that looks, from the outside and from the inside, like wisdom.

It helps to get specific about what that actually looks like. Not abstractly, concretely. Because you have been working toward a destination across this entire book, and you deserve to know what it is. And because knowing the destination changes how you see the small moments along the way, the patience you bring to a hard conversation, the repair you offer after losing your temper, the autonomy you extend when everything in you wants to just fix it.

The person you are building.

The Portrait: What High EQ Looks Like in Practice

They can name what they are feeling, with precision.

Not "fine." Not "stressed" used as an all-purpose weather report for any difficult internal state. They have both the vocabulary and the habit of self-examination to identify what is actually happening inside them with some specificity.

They know the difference between tired and sad, and they know that conflating them produces the wrong response to both. They know the difference between anxious and excited, which are physiologically nearly identical but point toward opposite interventions. They know the difference between defensive and hurt, and they know that when they are being defensive, it is almost always because they are actually hurt, and that knowing this changes how they respond to situations that trigger it.

This sounds small. It is enormous in practice. Because you cannot manage what you have not named. You cannot communicate clearly what you have not identified. You cannot ask for what you need if you do not know what you are experiencing.

The person who can say, in the middle of a hard conversation, "I am feeling defensive right now, which usually means I am actually feeling threatened or hurt about something, let me take a minute" is in a completely different relationship with their own inner life than the person who simply snaps and then wonders, afterward, why that keeps happening. The first person has agency. The second is being operated by their nervous system.

They take accountability without collapsing.

When they make a mistake, and they do, because they are human and because life continues to offer ample opportunities for mistakes regardless of how high your EQ is, they own it. Specifically, fully, without the asterisks and qualifications that drain apologies of meaning.

They feel the discomfort of having gotten it wrong. They do not skip past that discomfort: it is doing its job, which is to mark the event as significant and motivate repair. But they do not spiral, either. They do not spend three days in elaborate self-recrimination that is about managing their own guilt rather than addressing the person they hurt.

They own it, repair it, extract the lesson, and move forward. The cycle completes. They do not carry the accumulated, unprocessed weight of a thousand old mistakes that were never fully resolved, which is what compulsive self-criticism actually produces in the people who practice it.

They can sit with someone else's pain.

When someone they love is suffering, they do not immediately reach for a solution. They do not minimize. They do not pivot to their own related experience. They do not perform sympathy from a comfortable emotional distance.

They can stay present. They can say "I am here" and mean it physically, emotionally, and relationally, I am not going anywhere, I am not rushing you through this, I am not doing this because I have to and hoping it will be over soon.

They have the empathy to understand what is being experienced and the regulation to not be demolished by it. They can be moved without being swept away. And the person receiving their presence feels, in a way that is both hard to describe and unmistakable when it is present, genuinely accompanied.

They set and hold limits with warmth.

Their no is clear without being cruel. Their yes is genuine, not obligated. They know, from experience, not just in theory, the difference between being kind and being a doormat, and they have stopped confusing the two.

They give generously. But the generosity is real, because it comes from genuine choice. When they help someone, it is because they want to, and the person receiving the help can feel the difference between that and help that is given under the pressure of not being able to say no.

Their relationships have the quality that only relationships between genuinely autonomous people can have: a mutual recognition that both parties are choosing to be here. That neither is trapped. That the staying is voluntary, which is what makes it worth something.

They know the difference between reacting and responding.

The pause is not always perfect. High emotion still occasionally hijacks the best-regulated nervous system. They still sometimes say the thing they wish they had not said, still sometimes escalate when they intended to de-escalate, still sometimes need to come back afterward and repair.

But they catch it faster than they used to. They come back after they have regulated. The ratio of reactions to responses has shifted significantly in favor of responses. And crucially: when they do react, they know what happened. They can trace the activation, name the trigger, understand why that particular thing hit that particular nerve. That self-knowledge shortens the recovery and reduces the likelihood of the same reaction in the same situation next time.

They repair instead of abandon.

When relationships get difficult, when rupture happens, as it will in every relationship of any depth and duration, they move toward rather than away. Not because conflict is comfortable, but because they have enough experience of navigating conflict and coming out the other side with something intact or strengthened that they trust the process.

They have the skills. They know how to stay regulated enough to remain in the conversation. They know how to name what they are experiencing without attacking the other person. They know how to hear something hard without immediately defending against it. They know that repair is not the same as winning, and that the relationship matters more than being right.

And they do the repair explicitly, they do not simply let time pass and assume that the relationship has quietly restored itself. They come back. They check in. They say the thing out loud: we had a hard moment, and I am still here, and I want us to be okay.

They are genuinely curious about people unlike them.

Not tolerant: which is a low bar that essentially means enduring difference without visible complaint. Genuinely curious. They find different backgrounds, experiences, beliefs, and ways of moving through the world interesting rather than threatening.

They ask real questions and listen to the answers rather than waiting to rebut. They update their understanding when they encounter evidence that their model was incomplete. They hold their own perspective firmly enough to engage meaningfully and loosely enough to be genuinely changed by a conversation.

This is the long harvest of years of perspective-taking practice. Not just the ability to understand other people's experiences as an intellectual exercise, but the genuine interest in doing so: the orientation toward difference as something worth understanding rather than something to manage or avoid.

They fail without it becoming a crisis of identity.

Setbacks are events, not verdicts. Failure is information, not proof of inadequacy. When things do not work out, and they will not, regularly, because that is how life actually operates, they process the disappointment, extract what is useful to learn, and re-engage.

They do not need everything to go well in order to feel okay. Their sense of their own worth is not contingent on current performance. They can be struggling and still be fine in the more important sense, still grounded in a genuine sense of who they are that exists independently of whether today went well.

This is what decades of growth-mindset practice and debrief conversations and brave-mistake celebrations accumulate into: a person who is not fragile in the face of ordinary life difficulty. Who can be knocked down and get back up without a crisis about whether they are fundamentally okay.

The Things That Will Not Show Up on a Resume

Our culture has built an elaborate measurement infrastructure for cognitive intelligence and professional competence. Standardized tests. Grades. Portfolios. Performance reviews. Credentialing systems. All of them measuring something real and something limited.

We have almost nothing for measuring what this book has been about.

There is no standardized test for the ability to repair a relationship after conflict. No GPA for accountability. No credential for the capacity to sit with someone else's pain without rushing to fix it. No performance review category for the ability to identify what you are feeling and choose your response to it rather than simply enacting it.

But ask any hiring manager of genuine discernment what actually differentiates good employees from great ones: not in the interview, but over years of working together. Ask any couples therapist what the clients who successfully navigate the hard periods have that the clients who do not are missing. Ask any person over sixty what they wish they had developed earlier in their life, or what they would want most for their grandchildren.

It is almost never a higher test score. It is almost always some version of what we have been calling emotional intelligence: the capacity to know yourself, to manage yourself, to understand others, and to navigate relationships with some combination of skill and genuine care.

The work in this book does not show up on a transcript. It shows up everywhere else. It shows up in the quality of every relationship your child will ever have, every team they will ever work on, every hard conversation they will ever need to navigate, every loss they will ever need to survive and recover from.

NOTICE + NAME + REGULATE + CONNECT + REPAIR: What You've Built At Each Stage

THE BUILDER (Ages 2–5): The foundation you laid with a Builder is invisible and irreplaceable. You built the emotional climate of their earliest years: the texture of felt safety that determines whether the world is a place where feelings are okay or a place where they must be managed and hidden. They will not remember the specific moments, but they carry them. Every validation, every calm response to their storm, every "I see you and you're safe" is built into the architecture of who they are.

THE EXPLORER (Ages 6–10): The Explorer years are when the skills become visible. You can watch the vocabulary expand, the check-in habit take root, the debrief question start to run without prompting. This is the window where the investment has the clearest return: where the work you did in the Builder years produces recognizable capacity. Invest heavily here. The Explorer who leaves this stage with all Five Roots developing has an extraordinary foundation for everything ahead.

THE QUESTIONER (Ages 11–13): The Questioner years are when everything you built gets stress-tested for the first time. Apparent regression is normal. The capacity you built does not disappear: it goes underground while the developmental reorganization happens. Stay in the relationship. Keep the channels open even when they seem blocked. The Questioner who arrives at the Architect stage with the relationship intact, and with the sense that you have been genuinely curious about them even when they were difficult, has something most teenagers do not.

THE ARCHITECT (Ages 14–17): The Architect is integrating everything, building the identity that will carry them into adulthood, deciding which parts of what they learned at home are actually theirs. This is not rejection. This is the developmental project working correctly. Your job is to stay available, stay regulated, and resist the urge to control the integration. The values they internalize at this stage are genuinely theirs. That is the point. That is what you were building toward.

THE LAUNCHER (Ages 18–22): Here it is. The harvest. The young adult who can name what they're feeling, hold someone else's pain without being destroyed by it, own a mistake cleanly, set a boundary with warmth, repair a rupture rather than abandon a relationship, that person did not arrive fully formed. They were built, in ordinary moments, over years. By you. The relationship you have with them now, the one where they call you not because they have to but because they want to, is the long return on the whole investment. It is worth everything it cost.

On Letting Go: The Final Job

Nobody tells you this when you are standing in the delivery room holding something impossibly small and impossibly dependent:

The whole point is to make yourself unnecessary.

Every year, the goal is to be needed a little less in the practical sense, a little more in the optional sense: the sense of being someone your child wants to be in relationship with, chooses to call, finds genuinely interesting and genuinely comforting, rather than the person who manages and directs and solves.

Every skill you build in your child is a transfer of capacity from you to them. Every hard thing you let them navigate without fixing is an investment in their self-efficacy. Every repair you model and every accountability you demonstrate and every time you stay curious when judgment would have been easier, all of it is building the version of them that does not need you to do those things for them anymore.

The child who leaves home with robust emotional intelligence, a reliable sense of their own values, the skills to maintain and repair relationships, and the resilience to fail and recover, that child does not need you to manage their emotional life. They can do it. And the relationship that replaces the managerial one, the one between two capable adults who love each other and choose to remain in each other's lives, is one of the genuinely extraordinary things available to a human being.

It does not happen automatically. It is built, deliberately and imperfectly and repeatedly, over years of exactly the kind of work this book describes.

A man named Paul described his daughter, now twenty-seven, coming home after a painful breakup. She had been with someone for three years. It had ended badly. He had expected the version of homecoming he remembered from his own twenties: the falling apart, the needing to be talked off the ledge, the parent-as-crisis-manager dynamic that had defined his relationship with his own parents when things went wrong. That is not what happened. She came in, sat at the kitchen table, and talked for two hours. Not just about the relationship, about herself. What she had wanted from it and hadn't gotten. What she had provided and whether she'd been honest about her needs. What she had learned about what she was looking for and what she wasn't willing to compromise on. She cried. She laughed. She analyzed it with a clarity that he found genuinely striking. At the end she said, "I think I need about a month of not dating anyone, and then I'll be okay." He had not advised her once. He had not tried to fix it. He had just listened. Driving home afterward, he thought about all the years of hard conversations, all the times he and his wife had stayed in the room when leaving would have been easier, all the repairs, all the small moments of naming feelings and staying regulated and making space for honesty. He thought: that is what that was for. He called his wife from the car and told her. She cried a little. He did too.

The Five Roots at a Glance

Twelve chapters. Hundreds of small moments. One architecture. Here is what you built.

Root	The Skill	What It Looks Like in a High-EQ Adult
NOTICE	Emotional awareness	Catches their own activation early. Knows what they're feeling before it runs them.
NAME	Emotional vocabulary	Says "I'm embarrassed" not "I'm fine." Uses precision rather than burying the signal in vague noise.
REGULATE	The pause	Chooses their response. Doesn't eliminate emotion, creates space between feeling and action.
CONNECT	Empathy and belonging	Enters other people's experience rather than managing it from a safe distance. Builds trust.
REPAIR	Accountability and resilience	Owns mistakes cleanly. Moves toward rupture rather than away from it. Completes the cycle.

These five roots do not develop in sequence. They grow in relationship with each other, NOTICE feeds NAME, NAME enables REGULATE, REGULATE makes genuine CONNECT possible, and REPAIR is what happens when all four are working together under pressure.

A child with deep roots does not need favorable conditions to thrive. They carry the conditions with them.

Emotionally intelligent adults are not born. They are built. And you just built one.

That is what you built. That is the whole child.

TOOLS FOR CHAPTER TWELVE

The EQ Portrait Write down what you hope your child looks like emotionally at twenty-five. Not career, not achievement, not what they have: who they are and how they move through the world. How they handle failure. How they repair conflict. How they give and receive care. How they know themselves. This portrait is your parenting north star. When you are uncertain what to do in a difficult moment, ask: what response moves my child toward that portrait?

The Letting Go Inventory Identify one thing you are currently doing for your child that they are capable of doing for themselves. Transfer it. Offer support without solving. Notice both what they do with the responsibility and what you feel in the process of stepping back. Both are useful data.

The Long View Letter Write a letter to your child, not necessarily to give them, though you may choose to, describing the person you can already see them becoming. The qualities that are already present in embryonic form. The strengths you observe. The ways they already demonstrate the capacities this book has been building. Read it periodically when the daily reality of parenting is grinding. It keeps the long game visible when the short game is loud.

The Relationship Inventory Once a year, ask yourself honestly: what is the quality of my relationship with my child right now? Not their behavior: the relationship. Is there genuine warmth and genuine trust? Are there things they are not telling me that I wish they would? What would need to change for the relationship to be what I want it to be in ten years? The inventory, done honestly, points toward the specific work that most needs doing.

CONCLUSION

The Most Important Thing You Will Ever Build

We end where we began: with the adults.

Not the children, the adults. The ones you know and see every day. The ones in your workplace and your neighborhood and your family. The ones who are brilliant and capable and fundamentally decent and still somehow struggling with the things that matter most, their marriages, their mental health, their ability to handle difficulty without either exploding or shutting down, their capacity to be genuinely present with the people they love.

Look at them with clarity and without judgment. They are not struggling because they are not smart enough. They are not struggling because they did not work hard enough or want it badly enough. They are struggling because somewhere along the way, in some combination of the families they grew up in, the culture they were formed by, and the gaps that nobody noticed or addressed, they never fully built the internal infrastructure that life actually requires.

They do not have reliable access to what they are feeling. They cannot regulate well under pressure. They deflect accountability and cannot understand why their relationships keep failing. They cannot tolerate someone else's pain without rushing to fix it or flee it. They were never taught that failure is information rather than verdict, and so every significant setback feels like a verdict, and the weight of those accumulated verdicts is significant.

They are not bad people. They are people with gaps. And those gaps were, almost entirely, preventable.

You now have a blueprint for preventing them.

What This Work Actually Takes

Honesty is required about what implementing this blueprint requires, because it is not nothing and it deserves to be named clearly.

It takes honesty. Honest self-examination about your own emotional patterns: where they come from, how they are being transmitted, which ones you are proud of and which ones you would rather not pass on. This is not comfortable work. The chapters on modeling are the hardest ones for most parents to read, because they require looking at yourself with the same curious, non-judgmental attention you are trying to bring to your child.

It takes consistency. The skills in this book are built through repetition across years, not delivered in a single perfect conversation. The validation practice, the debrief habit, the repair after rupture, the accountability modeling: these work because they are done repeatedly, in small moments, until they become the normal texture of how your family operates. One excellent conversation does not build emotional intelligence. A thousand ordinary ones do.

It takes repair. You will get it wrong. Regularly. You will lose your patience when the situation called for regulation. You will lecture when you intended to listen. You will react when you meant to respond. This is not failure: it is the normal condition of trying to build something difficult while also being a human being with your own nervous system and history and tired moments.

What matters after you get it wrong is that you come back. That you repair explicitly, not by simply moving on and hoping the rupture healed itself. That you say, out loud: I handled that badly. I am sorry. Here is what I wish I had done instead. The repair is not the failure: it is the curriculum.

It takes the long view. Almost nothing in this book produces visible results quickly. The validation practice does not immediately produce a calmer child. The accountability modeling does not immediately produce an accountable one. The values conversations do not immediately produce a teenager with a solid moral architecture. The seeds take years to become visible. In some cases, you will not see the harvest until your children are adults and you watch how they navigate their own lives. The long game requires faith: the faith that the small moments accumulate into something real, even when the evidence is not yet visible.

Not perfect. Not composed at all times. Not cheerful through the difficulty. Just persistent, honest, and genuinely trying.

That is enough. That is more than enough. That is, in fact, what your children need from you more than any specific technique or framework this book has offered.

This Is Not Linear

One more thing worth saying plainly: emotional intelligence does not develop in a straight line, and neither does your relationship with your child.

There will be periods of apparent regression: the eight-year-old who had been naming feelings beautifully who suddenly has nothing to say about their inner life. The teenager whose values seem to have been entirely replaced by the values of whatever peer group currently has their attention. The child who owned mistakes readily at ten and now deflects everything at fourteen.

These are not failures of the work you have done. They are the normal oscillations of development: the two-steps-forward-one-step-back rhythm of a human being figuring out who they are. The capacity is being built even when it is not visible. The seeds are in the ground even when nothing has broken the surface.

What you have built does not disappear during the difficult periods. It waits. And when the developmental moment shifts, when the teenager's identity consolidation moves to a new phase, when the child's nervous system settles after a period of stress, when the young adult starts to integrate everything they have been given, what was built is there. Available. Real.

Stay in it. Keep showing up. The work is not wasted.

What You Were Actually Building

Twelve chapters. Hundreds of small practices. One through-line.

Every chapter in this book was developing one or more of the Five Roots: the foundational capacities that together constitute a person who can navigate actual life with skill, resilience, and integrity.

When you named your child's feeling out loud instead of dismissing it, you were building NOTICE.

When you reached for a more specific word than "upset," you were building NAME.

When you took a breath before walking into a hard conversation, you were building REGULATE, and modeling it.

When you stayed present with your child's pain instead of rushing to fix it, you were building CONNECT.

When you came back after losing your temper and said the thing out loud, you were building REPAIR.

None of it was small. None of it was wasted. The roots grow in the dark, invisibly, for years, and then one day you watch your child handle something hard and you see exactly what you built.

That moment is coming. Keep going until it arrives.

The Ripple Forward

The last thing, and perhaps the most important:

Emotional intelligence is transgenerational.

Children raised with high EQ become adults with high EQ. Adults with high EQ become parents with high EQ. They raise children with high EQ, who become parents, who raise children. The ripple moves forward through time in ways that are genuinely impossible to fully trace or measure.

Equally, the emotional damage of previous generations moves forward: the unprocessed grief, the unexamined patterns, the defensive behaviors that were once adaptive and are no longer, the gaps that nobody addressed because nobody knew how. It all moves forward, until someone interrupts it.

You are that interruption.

Every intentional choice you make, every time you choose curiosity over judgment, repair over silence, accountability over deflection, honesty over comfort, you are breaking a chain that may have been running for generations. You are building something that did not exist in the family before you. You are giving your children something you may not have fully received yourself.

That is not a small thing. That is an extraordinary thing. And it is worth every hard conversation, every imperfect repair, every moment of choosing the longer, harder, truer path when the shorter one was available.

Emotionally intelligent adults are not born. They are built. You are the builder.

Go build something extraordinary.

APPENDIX

Tools, Scripts, and Quick-Reference Cards

Everything in this appendix is drawn directly from the chapters. Use it as a field guide: the place to look when you are in the middle of something and need the distilled version without rereading the chapter.

Organized by **The Five Roots** so you can go directly to the skill you need.

NOTICE: Awareness Tools

Quick Reference: Age-by-Age EQ Milestones

Ages 2–4: Basic emotion vocabulary emerging. Tantrums are neurologically normal: not manipulation. Co-regulation by caregivers is the only available tool. The caregiver's regulated nervous system is the regulatory scaffold.

Ages 5–7: More nuanced emotional vocabulary developing. Beginning theory of mind and perspective-taking. The understanding that emotions and behavior are separate starts to form. Validation and simple emotion labeling are the primary tools.

Ages 8–10: Can reflect on emotional experiences after the fact, with some distance. Growing capacity for self-regulation with adult support. Empathy becomes more sophisticated and more consistent. The accountability script becomes genuinely teachable.

Ages 11–13: Puberty produces heightened emotional intensity. Peer relationships become central to identity. Both autonomy and connection are genuine needs simultaneously: not competing, both real. The digital conversation becomes important. Shame-based parenting becomes increasingly counterproductive.

Ages 14–17: Identity consolidation is the primary developmental project. Values-based motivation grows increasingly central and increasingly powerful. Self-regulation is still maturing: the environment and the relationship continue to matter enormously. Hold the line on the non-negotiables; increase the autonomy everywhere else.

Ages 18 and up: Integration. Skills built across childhood become internalized habits rather than performed behaviors. Repair and accountability become genuine rather than compliance. Empathy extends to increasingly diverse others. The relationship between parent and child begins its transition toward the one you have been building toward.

The Dinner Table Questions

Rotate through these regularly. The goal is not to get a specific answer: it is to build the habit of checking in with your inner life and sharing it with the people who matter. Start with yourself.

- What was the hardest part of today?
- What did you do for someone else today?
- Did anything surprise you?
- What feeling showed up the most for you today?
- Is there anything bothering you that you have not said yet?
- What are you proud of from today?
- Did you make any brave mistakes this week?

- What did you learn from something that went wrong?

NAME: Vocabulary Tools

Quick Reference: Shame vs. Guilt Language

The distinction that matters: guilt says "I did something wrong." Shame says "I am wrong." Build accountability through guilt. Avoid activating shame.

Instead of this (shame)	Say this (guilt)
"You are so irresponsible."	"That was an irresponsible choice. What happened?"
"I cannot believe you would do that."	"That behavior is not okay. Help me understand it."
"You always do this."	"This is the third time this week. Something is going on: what is it?"
"You are so sensitive."	"You feel things deeply. That is a real strength. Let us talk about this."
"You are being ridiculous."	"I can see you are really upset. Let us slow down."
"What is wrong with you?"	"Something got away from you there. Let us figure out what."

REGULATE: Regulation Tools

Quick Reference: The Conflict Resolution Framework

Step 1: Pause and regulate. No one resolves conflict well while flooded. Build in a mandatory cool-down, ten minutes minimum for children, thirty for teenagers and adults.

Step 2: Each person speaks without interruption. Use "I" statements. Describe your experience, not the other person's character.

Step 3: The listener reflects back. Before responding, demonstrate that you received what was said. "What I hear you saying is..."

Step 4: Identify underlying needs. Not positions (what you want), needs (why you want it). Needs are more often compatible than positions.

Step 5: Brainstorm solutions together. No evaluation during brainstorm. Put everything on the table, then evaluate.

Step 6: Agree, follow through, check in. State the agreement explicitly. Build in a follow-up: "Let us see how this is working in a few days."

Quick Reference: The Gottman Four Horsemen

Know them. Name them. Interrupt them in yourself and gently in your children.

Criticism: Attacking the person, not the behavior. Antidote: Complaint about the specific behavior, not the character.

Contempt: Communicating superiority or disgust. Eye-rolling, mockery, sarcasm as a weapon. Antidote: A consistent culture of appreciation and respect that survives disagreement.

Defensiveness: Treating every critique as an attack. Counter-blaming. Antidote: Find any piece of the feedback that is accurate. Take even partial responsibility.

Stonewalling: Shutting down, withdrawing. Antidote: Recognize flooding early. Ask explicitly for a break with a commitment to return.

CONNECT: Connection Tools

Quick Reference: The Validation Formula

Before any redirect, lesson, or consequence, validate first.

The structure: "I can see you are feeling [name the specific emotion, angry, scared, hurt, embarrassed]. That makes sense because [name the specific reason, what happened, what they lost, what felt unfair]. I am here."

Examples in practice: "I can see you are feeling really angry right now. That makes sense, you worked hard on that and it did not go the way you hoped. I am here." "I can see you are feeling left out. That makes sense: it hurts when friends make plans without you. I am here." "I can see you are feeling scared. That makes sense: this is new and you do not know how it will go. I am here."

The rule: Validation is not agreement. You are acknowledging the emotional experience as real and understandable. You are not endorsing every behavior that follows from it. These are separate conversations.

What not to say first: - "You should not feel that way." - "It is not a big deal." - "Other kids do not react like this." - "But you need to understand that..."

Say those things, if they need to be said, after the validation: not before it and not instead of it.

REPAIR: Accountability Tools

Quick Reference: The Accountability Script

Ages 4–7: Three questions. Practice them until they are automatic. 1. What did I do? 2. How did it make them feel? 3. What can I do to fix it?

Ages 8–12: The five-step apology framework. 1. Name specifically what you did: not "what happened," what you did. 2. Take full responsibility. No "but." No context. Just: I did this. 3. Acknowledge the impact. What was it like for them? 4. State what you will do differently. Specifically. 5. Follow through. The follow-through is the proof.

Teenagers: Same framework, with added nuance. Distinguish behavior from identity, explicitly and consistently. "What you did was wrong" is a very different statement from "you are someone who does wrong things." Acknowledge both that teenagers can handle being held accountable and that the way they are held accountable matters enormously for whether they learn from it or just survive it.

All Five Roots

The High-EQ Parenting Commitments

Read these periodically. They are the distilled practice of everything in this book. Not a checklist: a compass. Return to them when you have lost your bearings.

I will validate feelings before redirecting behavior.

I will own my mistakes out loud, in front of my children, and repair the ones that affected them.

I will make honesty safer than deception in our home.

I will praise effort and process more than outcome.

I will let my children experience manageable difficulty without rescuing them.

I will model the emotional skills I want them to develop, knowing they are watching everything.

I will repair every significant rupture, especially the ones I caused.

I will ask "what did you learn?" more often than "what happened?"

I will stay curious when it would be easier to judge.

I will protect my children's intrinsic motivations from my well-intentioned reward systems.

I will take their boundaries as seriously as I want them to take others'.

I will have the conversations about values, feelings, conflict, and mistakes during the calm moments so they are available in the hard ones.

I will remember, always, that the goal is capable adults, not compliant children.

Start Here Tonight

You finished the book. Here is where to begin.

Not all twelve chapters at once. Not a new system starting Monday. Tonight.

If your child is 2–5 (The Builder): At bedtime, narrate one feeling out loud: *"I felt really happy when we played together today."* No lesson. No follow-up. Just the words. That's it.

If your child is 6–10 (The Explorer): Ask one question at dinner: *"What was the hardest part of today?"* Don't fix it. Don't advise. Just listen and say, *"That sounds hard. Thanks for telling me."*

If your child is 11–13 (The Questioner): Say one true thing about yourself first: *"I felt frustrated today when something didn't go my way. I almost snapped at someone I shouldn't have."* No follow-up required. Just let it land.

If your child is 14–17 (The Architect): Find a side-by-side moment, driving, walking, doing something together, and ask without agenda: *"How are you actually doing?"* Then be quiet and mean it.

If your child is 18–22 (The Launcher): Send a message. Not advice. Not a check-in disguised as advice. Just: *"Thinking of you. No need to respond."* Let the relationship breathe.

The one practice that applies at every stage:

The next time your child is upset, try this before anything else:

"I can see you're [name the feeling]. That makes sense. I'm here."

That's the whole move. Validate before you redirect. Name before you fix. Stay before you solve.

Everything else in this book builds on that one moment, done thousands of times, across years.

Start tonight.

SELECTED SOURCES AND FURTHER READING

The research and frameworks referenced throughout this book draw on the following foundational works and researchers. This is not an exhaustive bibliography: it is a starting point for readers who want to go deeper.

On emotional intelligence and self-awareness Goleman, Daniel. *Emotional Intelligence: Why It Can Matter More Than IQ*. Bantam Books, 1995. Barrett, Lisa Feldman. *How Emotions Are Made: The Secret Life of the Brain*. Houghton Mifflin Harcourt, 2017. Brackett, Marc. *Permission to Feel: Unlocking the Power of Emotions to Help Our Kids, Our Colleagues, and Ourselves Thrive*. Celadon Books, 2019.

On emotion labeling and the brain Lieberman, Matthew D., et al. "Putting Feelings into Words: Affect Labeling Disrupts Amygdala Activity in Response to Affective Stimuli." *Psychological Science*, 2007.

On interoception and body-based emotional awareness Garfinkel, Sarah N., and Hugo D. Critchley. "Interoception, Emotion and Brain: New Insights Link Internal Physiology to Social Behaviour." *Social Cognitive and Affective Neuroscience*, 2013.

On mindset and learning from mistakes Dweck, Carol S. *Mindset: The New Psychology of Success*. Random House, 2006. Moser, Jason S., et al. "Mind Your Errors: Evidence for a Neural Mechanism Linking Growth Mind-Set to Adaptive Posterror Adjustments." *Psychological Science*, 2011.

On self-regulation and the window of tolerance Siegel, Daniel J. *The Developing Mind: How Relationships and the Brain Interact to Shape Who We Are*. Guilford Press, 1999. Siegel,

Daniel J., and Mary Hartzell. *Parenting from the Inside Out*. Tarcher/Penguin, 2003. Gross, James J. "Emotion Regulation: Affective, Cognitive, and Social Consequences." *Psychophysiology*, 2002.

On attachment and co-regulation Bowlby, John. *A Secure Base: Parent-Child Attachment and Healthy Human Development*. Basic Books, 1988. Ainsworth, Mary D.S., et al. *Patterns of Attachment: A Psychological Study of the Strange Situation*. Erlbaum, 1978. Main, Mary, and Judith Solomon. "Discovery of an Insecure-Disorganized/Disoriented Attachment Pattern." *Affective Development in Infancy*, 1986. Schore, Allan N. *The Science of the Art of Psychotherapy*. W.W. Norton, 2012.

On shame, guilt, and accountability Brown, Brené. *Daring Greatly*. Gotham Books, 2012. Tangney, June Price, and Ronda L. Dearing. *Shame and Guilt*. Guilford Press, 2002.

On empathy Goleman, Daniel, and Richard J. Davidson. *Altered Traits: Science Reveals How Meditation Changes Your Mind, Brain, and Body*. Avery, 2017. Kidd, David Comer, and Emanuele Castano. "Reading Literary Fiction Improves Theory of Mind." *Science*, 2013. Levinson, Wendy, et al. "Physician-Patient Communication: The Relationship with Malpractice Claims Among Primary Care Physicians and Surgeons." *JAMA*, 1997.

On conflict and relationships Gottman, John M., and Nan Silver. *The Seven Principles for Making Marriage Work*. Crown, 1999. Fisher, Roger, and William Ury. *Getting to Yes: Negotiating Agreement Without Giving In*. Penguin Books, 1981.

On motivation and autonomy Deci, Edward L., and Richard M. Ryan. *Intrinsic Motivation and Self-Determination in Human Behavior*. Plenum, 1985. Lepper, Mark R., David Greene, and Richard E. Nisbett. "Undermining Children's Intrinsic Interest with Extrinsic Reward." *Journal of Personality and Social Psychology*, 1973. Pink, Daniel H. *Drive: The Surprising Truth About What Motivates Us*. Riverhead Books, 2009.

On resilience and mistakes Mogel, Wendy. *The Blessing of a Skinned Knee*. Scribner, 2001. Bandura, Albert. *Self-Efficacy: The Exercise of Control*. W.H. Freeman, 1997.

On people-pleasing, self-compassion, and boundaries Brown, Brené. *The Gifts of Imperfection*. Hazelden, 2010. Neff, Kristin. *Self-Compassion: The Proven Power of Being Kind to Yourself*. William Morrow, 2011.

On screens, social media, and adolescent development Twenge, Jean M. *iGen: Why Today's Super-Connected Kids Are Growing Up Less Rebellious, More Tolerant, Less Happy*. Atria Books, 2017. Haidt, Jonathan. *The Anxious Generation: How the Great Rewiring of Childhood Is Causing an Epidemic of Mental Illness*. Penguin Press, 2024. Odgers, Candice L., and Michaeline R. Jensen. "Annual Research Review: Adolescent Mental Health in the Digital Age." *Journal of Child Psychology and Psychiatry*, 2020. Twenge, Jean M., et al. "Increases in Depressive Symptoms, Suicide-Related Outcomes, and Suicide Rates Among U.S. Adolescents After 2010." *Clinical Psychological Science*, 2018.

On temperament Chess, Stella, and Alexander Thomas. *Temperament in Clinical Practice*. Guilford Press, 1986. Aron, Elaine N. *The Highly Sensitive Person*. Broadway Books, 1996.

ABOUT THE AUTHOR

Ken Konet, M.Ed., MBA is a Corporate Instructional Designer, learning scientist, and author whose work spans three decades of helping organizations and individuals understand how people actually learn, change, and grow.

Ken holds three master's degrees, an M.Ed. in instructional design, and two MBA's, (because one wasn't enough), and has spent his career designing the systems, curricula, and training programs that help adults acquire difficult skills efficiently. His professional background sits at the intersection of cognitive science, behavioral psychology, and practical application: understanding not just what people should do, but how to build the conditions and experiences that make the doing actually possible.

The Whole Child is the product of that professional lens applied to the most important learning environment most people will ever inhabit: the family. The same principles that govern how adults learn complex skills in organizational settings, modeling, practice, feedback, psychological safety, intrinsic motivation, govern how children develop emotional intelligence at home. Ken has spent years translating that research into something a real parent can use on a real Tuesday.

A significant part of Ken's corporate work has focused specifically on emotional intelligence, designing and delivering EQ-based curricula for adult professionals across industries, from frontline managers learning to have difficult conversations to senior leaders navigating organizational conflict and cultural change. That work revealed something important: the adults sitting in those training rooms who struggled most with the material were not lacking intelligence or motivation. They were working with a foundation that had never been built. The regulation skills, the empathy skills, the accountability skills, the ones the training was trying to install in professionals in their thirties and forties, were skills that should have been developed in childhood. *The Whole Child* is, in part, the upstream answer to a downstream problem Ken has spent decades watching organizations try to solve.

Ken is also a prolific author across fiction and nonfiction, with titles spanning leadership, productivity, human behavior, psychology, and genre fiction. He writes with the conviction that good ideas deserve to be communicated clearly, honestly, and without the artificial gravity that makes important books unreadable.

He lives in Florida with his wife, Izzy.

The Whole Child: Raising Emotionally Intelligent Kids in a World That Forgot How by: Ken Konet, M.Ed., MBA

-THE END-

www.ingramcontent.com/pod-product-compliance
Lightning Source LLC
LaVergne TN
LVHW030910080826
845145LV00010B/2840

* 9 7 8 1 9 6 6 7 0 3 2 9 7 *